The Farmer's Wife Cookbook

Martha Engstrom, Editor

The momentous question of "What shall we eat," which comes to the housekeeper three times every day and which must be met with a well-supplied table—whether everything else in the house goes undone—becomes monotonous and wearying. We hail suggestions as a ship-wrecked mariner does the distant sail.
—"Table Talk," *The Farmer's Wife*, May 1912

Voyageur Press

First published in 1996 by Voyageur Press, an imprint of MBI Publishing Company, 400 First Avenue North, Suite 300, Minneapolis, MN 55401 USA

Voyageur Press titles are also available at discounts in bulk quantity for industrial or sales-promotional use. For details write to Special Sales Manager at MBI Publishing Company, 400 First Avenue North, Suite 300, Minneapolis, MN 55401 USA.

To find out more about our books, join us online at www.voyageurpress.com.

Editor: Elizabeth Knight
Designer: Andrea Rud
Cover Design: JoDee Mittlestadt

Printed in China

Library of Congress Cataloging-in-Publication Data
Engstrom, Martha, 1950–
          The Farmer's Wife Cookbook / by Martha Engstrom.
                    p.   cm.
          Includes index.
          ISBN-13: 978-0-7603-3489-8
          ISBN-10: 0-7603-3489-7
          1. Cookery, American. I. Title.
    TX715.E579   1996
    6411.5973—dc20   96-11994

ACKNOWLEDGMENTS
The recipes in this book were chosen from *The Farmer's Wife*, a monthly magazine from Webb Publishing of St. Paul, Minnesota, and from *The Country Kitchen Cook Book*, first published in 1894 by *The Farmer's Wife*. The illustrations and cover art were also reproduced from *The Farmer's Wife*. My thanks to *Farm Journal* of Philadelphia, Pennsylvania, for permission to adapt and reproduce all materials.

Contents

THE
FARMER'S WIFE
A Magazine for Farm Women

Welcome to the Farm Kitchen

The recipes in *The Farmer's Wife Cookbook* are true farm recipes. They originated in country kitchens and were submitted by readers to *The Farmer's Wife,* a monthly magazine published from 1893 to 1939 by Webb Publishing Company of St. Paul, Minnesota. Many of these recipes are almost a century old, offering a step back in time to another era of cooking. They have all been updated for the modern kitchen to provide similar results today as they did in Grandma's kitchen.

Many of the recipes are downright delicious, such as the Swedish Meatballs, the pies and cakes. . . . Some are chock full of nostalgia, reviving memories of Grandma's special cooking. Others are quaint, offering a window to look back at a long-ago style of North American farm country cookery that is largely forgotten today.

Other than spices and such, the recipes call for the homegrown ingredients that were typically raised and produced on American farms during this era. Milk and cream, both sweet and sour, butter, chicken and eggs, cured meats, variety meats (today's vernacular for organs such as the heart and liver), and fresh and home-canned fruits and vegetables were considered staples. The recipes were created to give equally satisfying results using either fresh or preserved ingredients.

The Farmer's Wife Cookbook presents recipes for soups and salads, as well for as meat, egg, and vegetable dishes. Of course, no farm cookbook would be complete without recipes for baked and canned goods that were deemed "good enough" for county and state fair competitions. Included are recipes for pies, cakes, cookies, fudge, candied fruit, muffins, and breads—all of which were proudly submitted to *The Farmer's Wife* by their blue-ribbon-winning creators. Modern guides to home canning—with recipes for jams and jellies, pickles and relishes—are also included.

Most of the recipes in *The Farmer's Wife Cookbook* were planned for the average-sized family of an earlier era—from four to six persons. Some are written in generous quantities that allow for second helpings or leftovers. If you reduce or increase a recipe, note the amounts of ingredients used for future reference.

In reviewing issues from almost forty years of *The Farmer's Wife,* I was struck by the number of feature articles and fictional works that touched on the significance of "community." The desire or need for farm families to participate in both social events and common work-related activities, within the greater community, was an everyday, embracing theme. The purpose or focus of such gatherings varied, but common to all was *food.* Whether it was a church circle or some other women's society, the 4-H club, or the crews of men who aided neighbors in raising barns or threshing grain, a meal to be shared by all participants was considered central to the event or activity itself.

First Courses and Soups

First courses or appetizers are meant to stimulate the appetite and put one in a frame of mind to enjoy a meal. For that reason, something light and refreshing is the rule, such as fruit in some form, a light soup, or canapés. Sometimes a crisp salad of fresh fruits or green vegetables is served as the first course.

Fruit cups, fruit juice, sea food, or tomato cocktails should be served cold. Keep fruit in fairly large, distinct pieces—not mushy, and not sweetened to excess. Fruit punch makes an attractive and appetizing first course when served in tall glasses or sherbet cups.

Soup served as a first course should be light, such as a clear broth with a few vegetables or bouillon. Cream soups, chowders, and rich vegetable soups serve as the main course of a supper or luncheon. Then generous bowls can be served, while first-course soups are served in small soup plates or cups.

—*The Farmer's Wife*

Fruits

Winter Fruit Cup

Serves 8–10

½ cup (125 ml) honey or ⅓ cup (80 ml) sugar
½ cup (125 ml) water
Juice of ½ lemon
4 oranges, pared and diced
4 bananas, diced, or 1 cup (250 ml) canned pears
4 apples, cored and diced
2 cups (500 ml) diced pineapple, or 2 cups (500 ml) canned peaches
1 cup (250 ml) red grapes

1. Make a syrup of the honey or sugar and the water by combining and heating in a saucepan. Stir continuously and allow to boil for 3–4 minutes. Add the lemon juice. Cool completely.
2. Prepare the fuit and put in a large bowl. Pour the syrup over the fruit. Mix gently. Refrigerate for 1 hour and serve.

Cranberry Cocktail

Serves 4

1 cup (250 ml) raw cranberries, halved
½ cup (125 ml) diced pineapple
1 cup (250 ml) raisins
1 cup (250 ml) pineapple juice
½ cup (125 ml) sugar

1. Combine the cranberries, diced pineapple, and raisins in a large bowl. Pour the sugar and juice over the fruit. Mix gently.
2. Cover and refrigerate overnight. Serve chilled.

Melon Cocktail

Combine balls or cubes of melon of two or three colors in sherbet glasses. Pour one of the following over the melon, cool, and serve:
❧ Syrup of ½ cup (125 ml) sugar and ½ cup (125 ml) water cooked together, and juice of ½ lemon or lime.
❧ Juice of canned pineapple.
❧ Ginger ale.

Soups

Beef Stock

Serves 6

The following recipe makes a clear stock. For a brown stock, brown half the meat in the fat marrow from the veal knuckle before simmering.

3 pounds (1½ kg) lean beef
¼ cup (60 ml) oil (optional)
3 pounds (1½ kg) veal knuckle, cracked
3 quarts (3 l) cold water
½ cup (125 ml) diced carrots
½ cup (125 ml) diced turnips
½ cup (125 ml) diced celery
2 teaspoons salt
1 teaspoon peppercorns
4 cloves
1 sprig parley
1 bay leaf

1. Cut the beef in 1-inch (2.5-cm) cubes; brown half in the oil if desired. Put both the meat and veal knuckle in the cold water and cover; bring to a simmer and maintain for about 4 hours. Remove any scum that forms.
2. Add the carrots, turnips, celery, and seasonings, and simmer for an additional 30 minutes or until the vegetables are tender.
3. The beef and bones may be removed, and the mixture served as a vegetable soup.
4. Or, the liquid may be strained off at once, clarified, and used as a clear broth or soup stock.

Vegetable Soup

Serves 4–6

1 cup (250 ml) diced carrots
1 cup (250 ml) diced turnips
1 cup (250 ml) diced celery, with leaves
1 cup (250 ml) diced onions
¼ cup (60 ml) oil
2 quarts (2 l) beef stock
2 cups (500 ml) diced potatoes
1 pint (500 ml) home-canned tomatoes
1 tablespoon chopped parsley
1 teaspoon salt
¼ teaspoon pepper
1 bay leaf

1. In a large saucepan, brown the carrots, turnips, celery, and onions in the oil.
2. Add the beef stock to the vegetables. Bring to a boil, then reduce the heat to a simmer. Cover and cook slowly for 20–25 minutes or until the vegetables are tender but not mushy.
3. Add the potatoes, tomatoes, parsley, and seasonings, and cook for another 10–15 minutes.
4. Serve the soup in flat soup plates.

Minestrone

Serves 4–6

1 clove garlic, chopped
1 small head cabbage, chopped
3–4 medium potatoes, cubed
½ pound (250 g) string or waxed beans, chopped
2 tablespoons chopped parsley
3 tablespoons olive oil
½ cup (125 ml) tomato paste
3–4 cups (750–1000 ml) beef stock
1 cup (250 ml) cooked elbow macaroni, drained
½ cup (125 ml) grated Parmesan cheese

1. In a large saucepan, brown the garlic, cabbage, potatoes, beans, and parsley in the oil.
2. Add the tomato paste and beef stock. Bring to a boil, then reduce the heat, cover, and simmer for 30 minutes or until the vegetables are cooked to your liking. Add additional stock, if necessary.
3. Add the cooked macaroni. Cover and heat until the macaroni is thoroughly heated.
4. Serve topped with the Parmesan cheese.

Bean Chowder

Serves 4–6

2 cups (500 ml) dried navy beans
2 onions, diced
1 large smoked ham hock
2 tablespoons oil
4 cups (1 l) home-canned tomatoes
2 tablespoons molasses or brown sugar
¼ teaspoon pepper
1 teaspoon salt

1. Cover the beans with cold water and soak overnight.
2. Drain the beans, place in a large soup kettle, and cover with fresh cold water. Bring to a boil, then reduce the heat, cover, and simmer gently.
3. In the oil, brown together the onions and smoked ham hock until the onions are soft.
4. Add the onions and ham hock to the beans. Continue to simmer until the beans are tender, approximately 1–1¼ hours, adding more water as necessary.
5. To give a smooth base to the chowder, remove a part of the beans, purée, and return to the pot.
6. Add the tomatoes, molasses, pepper, and salt. Simmer for 30 minutes longer.
7. Remove the ham hock and serve.

Variation

Split Pea Chowder: Substitute dried split peas for dried navy beans. Tomatoes are optional.

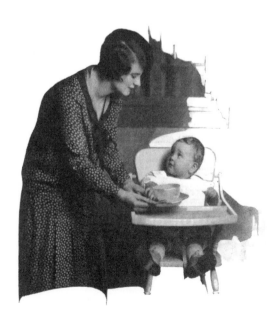

Approved by Farm Women

July 1936

If someone should offer you a guide to help you do a better job of buying, would you be interested?

Naturally you would. Probably few things would interest you more.

Well, on this page, *The Farmer's Wife* magazine presents for the first time a seal which will be just such a guide. It will become familiar to you in the months and years to come, and you will discover that it is a friendly emblem in which you can put trust.

New Reader-Test Approval Seal

Whenever you see the new Reader-Test Approval Seal of *The Farmer's Wife* magazine, you will know that the product on which it appears has been given an unbiased test by 100 to 500 farm women like you, in homes like yours, and has been approved by them for farm home use. This reader-test will supplement the manufacturer's own tests and still others made by our own trained foods editor in *The Farmer's Wife* Country Kitchen.

One homemaker to whom we explained this new idea said: "That would mean a lot to me—to know that women themselves have tried a product in their own homes and like it." And we believe that you will agree that this is the most valuable kind of test, from your standpoint, that any product could possibly have. For it will tell how it actually performs under all manner of farm home conditions, including yours. And that, after all, is what farm women buyers really want to know.

Choice of the "Reader-Testers"

To make these tests, we have selected a group of readers of *The Farmer's Wife* magazine to be "reader-testers." There will be 500 to begin with and perhaps more later. To make sure that some of them will be like you, with equipment like yours, we have chosen them so that they will give a complete cross section of American farm homes.

Take the first three women who enrolled in the reader-test group, for example. The first lives on a big dairy farm, has three children but cooks for a family of ten including hired help, and has a wood-burning range supplemented by a liquid-fuel stove.

The second has three children, five to twelve years old, and cooks on an electric range.

The third has children ranging from one in grade school to a married daughter living across the road. The daughter is just learning to cook, and both she and her mother, who is a splendid cook, will make the tests. They use a bottled gas range.

Still others use kerosene and gasoline stoves. Their families vary all the way from no children to ten. And the farms range all the way from truck acreages to ranches.

Not only will these homes vary widely in the experience of the homemaker, the size of family, and the kind of equipment, but they will be located in all parts of the country. And this is important, for tastes in food vary not only by families but by sections of the country (as witness the difference in opinion between North and South on whether there should be sugar in corn bread).

Opinions of Outstanding Women

But while there will be all of these variations, the women will have this in common: They will all be outstanding women in whom their neighbors have confidence. They will be alert women interested in keeping in touch with new developments in foods and equipment. And they will be independent thinkers, under no obligation to any one, who will give us their honest opinions no matter what they may be. In the reports, which these reader-testers send us on foods products, they will not only comment on the food preparation but on how the family liked the things prepared, thus giving the products both a preparation and an appetite test.

If their experience with the article is good—if they say, "I like this product, not only because it is of high quality but because it is practical for farm home use"—then *The Farmer's Wife* magazine will give the manufacturer permission to use our Reader-Test Approval Seal on the product itself and on his advertising of it.

The New Reader-Test Seal and What It Will Mean To You

Since this reader-test idea is brand new, it will be a few months before manufacturers can begin using it. We plan, however, that the Reader-Test Approval Seal, which you see on this page, will begin appearing in the advertising columns of *The Farmer's Wife* magazine, as well as in retail store displays, in manufacturers' cookbooks, and on the products themselves, within a few months.

The Farmer's Wife magazine has always carefully checked its editorial material to see that it is accurate, practical, and useful for farm homemakers. Two years ago we took a long forward step by establishing the Country Kitchen, where all recipes could be tested and approved before they were printed. Since then you have become familiar with the little triangle seal of the Country Kitchen in connection with these recipes.

Likewise the magazine has long recognized that its advertising must be just as trustworthy as its editorial content. That is why we print the advertising guarantee which you can find each month at the bottom of the editorial page.

Now we are adding our Reader-Test Approval Seal as a further guarantee. It will be a sign by which you can buy with confidence, for it has behind it both the integrity of a reputable manufacturer and the reputation of The Farmer's Wife magazine. Best of all, it has behind it the approval of a group of actual farm women who have tried it in their own homes and liked it.

And so, Madame, we introduce you to the triangle with the silhouette of the woman—the new approval seal backed by The Farmer's Wife magazine and our reader-test women.

Cream Soups

Add puréed, cooked vegetables to a thin white sauce in the proportion of ½–1 cup (125–250 ml) purée to 2 cups (500 ml) white sauce. Some people prefer an unthickened cream soup. In that case, add butter or a little cream to the scalded milk, and then combine with the vegetable purée.

Some raw vegetables such as spinach, water cress, and cabbage can be shredded or ground and added to the hot milk. Cook in the milk for 10 minutes and then add butter and flour rubbed together to thicken slightly.

Cream of Tomato Soup

Serves 4–6

Use as little baking soda as possible to neutralize the tomatoes. Acidic tomatoes take more soda, whereas some home-canned tomatoes may not need any. Always add the hot tomato to the hot milk rather than the milk to the tomato.

2 cups (500 ml) home-canned tomatoes
1 slice of onion
1 small bay leaf
¼ teaspoon baking soda
3 tablespoons butter
3 tablespoons flour
1 quart (1 l) milk
½ teaspoon salt
Pepper

1. Cook the tomatoes for 10 minutes with the slice of onion and bay leaf. Remove from the heat. Remove the bay leaf and purée the tomatoes (or mash them through a sieve). Add the baking soda and return to the heat.
2. In a separate saucepan, make a thin white sauce with the butter, flour, and milk and season with the salt and pepper.
3. Keep the white sauce hot, and just before serving, pour the tomatoes into the white sauce. Stir to combine. Serve at once.

Corn Chowder

Serves 4–6

6 slices bacon
3 onions, sliced
6 small potatoes, sliced
1 can whole-kernel corn, 28 ounces (784 g)
1 cup (250 ml) cream
Salt and pepper
1 cup (250 ml) diced ham
1 green pepper, chopped

1. Mince the bacon and fry in a deep skillet or casserole.
2. Add the onions; cover and cook for 15–20 minutes or until the onions are tender.
3. Add the potatoes and sufficient water to cover. Bring to a boil, then reduce the heat to a simmer. Cover and cook for another 20–25 minutes or until the potatoes are tender.
4. Add the corn and cream, and season with the salt and pepper to taste.
5. Add the ham and green pepper. Heat thoroughly and serve.

Hot Soups for Cold Days

by Mabel K. Ray, January 1934

When days are cold, steaming hot soup seems to "strike the spot" just a little better than anything else. Whether it is the clear soup that whets the appetite and is used as a starter for the meal to follow, or the more substantial soup that makes a whole meal in itself, there is a time and place for every soup. Besides, soups are economical and easy to do, offer perfect use for odds and ends of leftovers, and make the family—like Oliver Twist—come back asking for "more."

Soups, like dresses, are made more attractive by a bit of trimming. Some cream soups are as colorless and uninteresting as a dull-colored dress. A bit of paprika sprinkled over the top of each dish gives just that bit of dash that a red buckle can give to a colorless dress.

Choosing a Refrigerator

by Lucile W. Reynolds, May 1930

The slogan, a refrigerator for every home, is one that is frequently quoted. And those of us who use a refrigerator during the hot weeks in summer are quite ready to agree that it is a very essential piece of equipment. There are sections of the country where there are few days in the year in which refrigeration seems necessary. But in most sections of the United States there are at least two or three months in the year when a refrigerator adds much to our comfort and may even safeguard our health.

Granted, then, that a refrigerator is desirable, shall the housewife make her selection on the basis of gleaming white surfaces, "smooth-as-glass" linings or bright hardware—or are there more fundamental features to look for? Fortunately there are some rather definite standards to guide her in the choice of a cabinet, whether it is to be cooled by ice or by mechanical means.

Food Storage Space

The first consideration in purchasing a refrigerator is the size. What the housewife really wants is a cabinet with adequate food storage space in which to store the perishable foods for the everyday needs of her family as well as sufficient additional space to take care of special occasions such as threshers, harvest hands, and week-end guests. At least 5 cubic feet of food storage space is needed for a family of four. But for many farm families this would be far too small and a box with 7 or 9 cubic feet would better serve their needs. If the refrigerator is also to be used for the temporary storage of cream, butter, eggs, or other foods intended for market, this should be taken into consideration in deciding on the space needed. If your dealer cannot tell you the volume of the cabinet you are considering, you can easily measure the food storage compartment yourself and thus get a rough approximation of the space available.

We used to think that the way to purchase a refrigerator was on the basis of its ice capacity. Thus a woman thought that if she bought a "100-pound icer" she would have a generous amount of food storage space. Recently in a study of seven different refrigerators, each of which was rated as having an ice capacity of 100 pounds, it was found that the volume of space available for food storage varied from approximately 5 cubic feet in one cabinet to 8 cubic feet in another! So it is evident that it is not enough to know the ice capacity of the cabinet.

Better materials and better construction are found in the larger refrigerators. With one or two exceptions it is very difficult today to find on the market a well constructed small cabinet. Available space in the kitchen is a determining factor in deciding on the size to choose. But because rural homes are as a rule more spacious, this is less of a problem in the country than it is in town.

Insulation

Some form of insulation is an absolutely essential feature in the construction of a refrigerator cabinet. Its function is to act as a barrier and thus to prevent the warm air in the room from entering the refrigerator. The insulating material occupies the space between the outside wall of the cabinet and the lining. Formerly it was not considered necessary to fill in this space. It was argued that the air thus confined was dead air and that it was effective as insulation. Dead air is a good insulator. But it is practically impossible to keep the air that is confined in a space of this size from circulating. And circulating air is not dead air. So beware of the refrigerator which is recommended

to you because it is insulated with "dead air." Rather look for a cabinet that is insulated with cork board or some of the other good insulating materials in sheet or board form. Though the insulating value of many of these materials in granulated form is about the same as that of the same material when pressed into sheets or boards, the latter has the advantage in that it stays in place and does not settle.

How thick should the insulation be? The Bureau of Standards says that "an ordinary household refrigerator should have the equivalent of not less than 2 inches of insulation."

Some of the more progressive manufacturers have affixed a label on their refrigerators stating the kind and amount of insulation used in the construction. Many dealers have awakened to the fact that it is to their interest to carry in stock well-insulated cabinets. Your part, then,

is to insist that you be shown refrigerators which feature good insulation. If there is a label, read it carefully. Ask to see the manufacturer's catalog in which the special features of his product are discussed. And remember that if insulating material, adequate in kind and amount, is built into the cabinet and the ice compartment is kept at least half full of ice, it is possible to maintain a low temperature in the food compartment even in the hot days of summer.

Good Construction

Although the insulation cannot be seen, other essentials of good construction can be. The refrigerator is a piece of equipment that is to give service for a number of years. It needs to be sturdily built so that it will stand the strain. It should look substantial. The seams and joints should be fitted closely. If the exterior is of wood, a surface that is smooth is preferable to one that is panelled. The former means fewer seams and joints, consequently less opportunity for warm air from outside to enter the refrigerator. A cabinet set on legs is easier to clean under and necessitates less stooping. Are the doors as thick as the walls, suggesting that the same construction has been used throughout? Are the hinges and clasps strong and sturdy? They are a very important element of good construction. Modern refrigerator design includes a rubber gasket attached to the inner surface of the door. It is just another precaution to insure a close-fitting door.

Lining

The lining of the refrigerator should be of such a nature that it can easily be cleaned. It should be carefully constructed so that there are no cracks through which moisture from the inside of the box may get into the insulation, or in which decayed food may find a lodging. If there are seams, they should be well soldered. Solid porcelain is used for linings only in the very high-priced cabinets. Most of the cabinets on the market have a metal lining. In some of the cheaper cabinets, no finish is applied to the metal, although the tendency now is to apply some type of white enamel finish. As all housewives know, an enamel that is painted or baked on is more apt to chip and scratch than one which is fused on. However, if care is used, such a finish may be kept in good condition for several years. Insulating value is not greatly affected by the nature of the coating used on the lining nor the method by which it is applied. If a choice must be made between a cabinet which has an expensive lining but is poorly insulated and a well-insulated cabinet with a less attractive lining, by all means choose the latter.

Mechanically Cooled Refrigerator

The same principles which govern the selection of an ice-cooled cabinet also govern the selection of a mechanically cooled refrigerator. Whether the motor is located in the basement, under the refrigerator, or on top, whether the refrigerant is sulphur dioxide, ammonia, methyl chloride, or ice, the important thing to the housewife is to have a safe, convenient place for the storage of perishable foods when the thermometer registers 75° Fahrenheit (30° Celsius) or more. For this a well-constructed, adequately insulated cabinet is essential. The fact that dealers in mechanical units will not install them in cabinets that do not measure up to the standard outlined above suggests that the prospective purchaser of ice-cooled cabinets who hopes some time in the future to equip her cabinet with an electric unit will find these suggestions of immediate practical value.

Cost

It is superfluous to add that all of these features of good construction add to the cost of the cabinet. A high-grade cabinet is expensive. But less ice, less current, will be needed to operate it than one that is more cheaply built. The temperature in the food compartment will be lower. Hence food can be kept in satisfactory condition for a longer period. It will cost less to keep such a cabinet in good condition. If properly cared for it will have a longer life. In the end, then, it pays to purchase a high grade cabinet, but one must remember that price is not the only guide to quality.

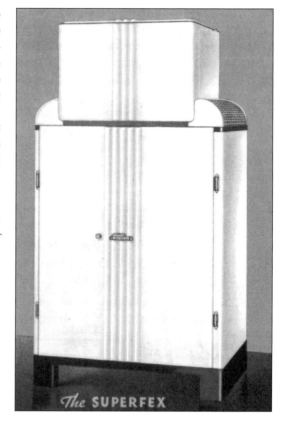

The SUPERFEX

Chapter 2

Beverages

Beverages are meant to refresh and stimulate. Sometimes a hot milk drink at bedtime helps one relax, but most beverages act as mild stimulants. Since we all need from one to two quarts of water daily to aid in regulating body processes, beverages help supply this amount.

As for food value, coffee and tea furnish no food value except through the trimmings which each person chooses for himself. Cocoa, chocolate, and other milk drinks are valuable as carriers of milk. When milk drinks are attractively served, children will usually accept them readily, even those who have expressed a dislike for milk. Avoid over-sweetening milk drinks, or a distaste for milk in its natural state may be developed. Fruit drinks are especially popular in the summer time. They are much more refreshing if not oversweet.

Anything in excess can be harmful, a rule which holds true in regard to coffee, tea, and cocoa. Properly made, these beverages contain less of the substances which can do harm (caffeine, tannin, and theo-bromine) than when brewed too long or too strong.
—*The Farmer's Wife*

Minted Tea

1½ quarts (1½ l) boiling water
2½ tablespoons orange pekoe tea
4 or 5 mint leaves
Mint leaves for garnish
Slices of orange

1. Pour the boiling water over the tea and mint leaves, and allow it to stand for 10 minutes.
2. Pour off the liquid, chill, and dilute or pour over cracked ice.
3. Serve with a fresh mint leaf and a slice of orange in each glass.

Fruit Tea Punch

2 tablespoons tea
2 cups (500 ml) boiling water
2 cups (500 ml) water
1 cup (250 ml) sugar
Juice of 3 lemons
Juice of 2 oranges
1 cup (250 ml) grated pineapple

1. Pour the freshly boiled water over the tea and let steep for 5 minutes.
2. Boil the 2 cups (500 ml) water with the sugar for 5 minutes and add the fruit juices and pineapple.
3. When the fruit juice mixture is cold, add the prepared tea and pour over cracked ice.

Fruit Fizz

Juice of 4 oranges
Juice of 2 lemons
½ cup (125 ml) unsweetened pineapple juice
1 cup (250 ml) maraschino cherries and juice
1 quart (1 l) sparkling white grape juice

1. In a large pitcher, combine the juice from the oranges and lemons with the pineapple juice, cherries, and cherry juice.
2. Add the sparkling grape juice immediately before serving.

Iced Coffee

Leftover coffee cannot be expected to make good iced coffee.

1. Make the coffee a little stronger than usual to allow for dilution by ice.
2. Pour the hot coffee over ice in individual glasses. Use powdered sugar for sweetening and cream as desired. It may be topped off with whipped cream.

Coffee Syrup

2 cups (500 ml) extra strong coffee
3½ pounds (1¾ kg) sugar

1. Boil 2–3 minutes. Pour in sterilized bottles and seal. Keeps indefinitely.

Cocoa Syrup

1 cup (250 ml) cocoa
3 cups (750 ml) sugar
¼ teaspoon salt
2 cups (500 ml) cold water
3 teaspoons vanilla

1. Mix the cocoa, sugar, salt, and water in a saucepan.
2. Place over a low flame, stirring constantly until the sugar is dissolved and the mixture boils. Boil uncovered for 5 minutes.
3. Add the vanilla and let cool.
4. Pour into a container and refrigerate.

Variations
Hot Cocoa: Heat the milk and add 1 tablespoon syrup for each cup (250 ml) of hot milk. Mix well until frothy. A marshmallow or spoonful of whipped cream makes a special topping for hot cocoa.
Iced Cocoa: Add enough cocoa syrup to flavor cold milk and beat briskly with an egg beater. For a special treat, top iced cocoa with a spoonful of whipped cream or ice cream and serve with straws.

Whey Lemonade

1 quart (1 l) whey
6 tablespoons sugar
Juice of 2 lemons
Slices of lemon or a little grated or diced rind
Nutmeg or cinnamon

Mix, chill, and serve.

Rhubarb Punch

1 quart (1 l) diced rhubarb
1 quart (1 l) water
Grated rind of 1 lemon or orange
¾–1 cup (185–250 ml) sugar

1. In an uncovered saucepan, simmer the rhubarb in the water for 10 minutes or until very tender.
2. Strain. Add the grated lemon and sugar, stirring until the sugar is dissolved.
3. Cool and chill on ice before serving.

Raspberry Mint

1 pint (500 ml) raspberries
½ cup (125 ml) sugar
¼ cup (60 ml) water
1 orange
12 fresh mint leaves
1 tablespoon lemon juice
mint sprigs for garnish

1. Place the raspberries in a saucepan, sprinkle with the sugar, and let stand for 1 hour.
2. Purée the raspberries. Add the water and bring to a boil.
3. Squeeze the juice from the orange and cut several long, thin strips of the rind.
4. Add the orange juice and rind, mint leaves slightly crushed, and lemon juice to the raspberries. Allow to boil uncovered for 5 minutes.
5. Cool, strain, and pour into a refrigerator tray. Freeze to a mush.
6. Serve with a sprig of fresh mint.

Spiced Grape Juice

1 quart (1 l) grape juice
¼ cup (60 ml) sugar
6 whole cloves
2 short pieces stick cinnamon
A few allspice berries
Additional cloves (garnish)

1. Heat the ingredients in a double boiler or over low heat. Do not boil. Strain out the spice.
2. Serve hot with a whole clove on top of each cup.

Beverages That Refresh *and* Something *to* Crunch

by Mabel K. Ray, July 1932

On a sweltering summer day, who wouldn't like a crispy something to crunch and a beverage with a clink of ice in it? Nothing, absolutely nothing, is more refreshing—or at least that is the way many feel about it.

And when you come to kinds of drinks, there is such a vast array that a different one could be served almost every day in the year. Fruit drinks, milk drinks, malt cocoa food drinks, chocolate and cocoa drinks, coffee drinks, and tea drinks are just a few of the appetizing ones.

To get the "crunch," cheese sticks, fattigmands, graham crackers, salted crackers, and other wafers meet the requirements. The recipes? Here they are!

Fattigmands

Ingredients
5 egg yolks
1 whole egg
6 tablespoons sugar
6 tablespoons whipping cream
1 teaspoon flavoring
1¾ cups (425 ml) flour (enough to roll)
Powdered sugar

1. Beat the eggs in a mixing bowl until light, add the sugar, then beat again.
2. Whip the cream and add to the eggs and sugar.
3. Then add the flavoring and flour as for cookies.
4. Roll the dough extremely thin, cut in diamond shapes. Make a slit in one point and slip the other end through.
5. Fry in hot lard (they fry fast). About four at a time is enough. Turn as they come up and take out. Dust with powdered sugar if you desire.

Marguerites

Ingredients
1 egg white
½ cup (125 ml) marshmallows, cut up
½ cup (125 ml) chopped nuts
Crackers

1. Heat the oven to 350°/175°C.
2. Beat the egg white until stiff in a bowl.
3. Add the marshmallows and nuts. Mix.
4. Drop a small spoonful of the mixture on individual crackers and bake until a glaze has formed on top. Serve strictly fresh.

Cheese Crackers

Ingredients
2 dozen salted crackers
¼ pound (100 g) grated cheese

1. Heat the oven to 350°F/175°C.
2. Spread the crackers with the grated cheese.
3. Bake until brown, for about 5 minutes. Serve hot or cold.

Spiced Lime Juice

¾ cup (185 ml) sugar
½ cup (125 ml) water
1 lemon rind, cut into thin strips
4 whole cloves
1 cinnamon stick
1-inch (2.5-cm) piece of ginger root
Juice of 4 limes
4 cups (1 l) ice water
Fresh mint sprigs

1. In a saucepan, combine the sugar, ½ cup (125 ml) water, lemon rind, cloves, cinnamon, and ginger root. Boil uncovered for 5 minutes.
2. Cool and add the lime juice.
3. Strain and add the ice water.
4. Serve with the fresh mint garnish.

Ambrosia

Juice of 3 oranges
Juice of 1 grapefruit
Juice of 1 lemon
¼ cup (60 ml) pineapple juice
5 maraschino cherries, chopped
1 slice pineapple, chopped
½ cup (125 ml) shredded coconut
1 cup (250 ml) sugar
3 cups (750 ml) water

1. In a large pitcher, combine the juice from the oranges, grapefruit, and lemon with the pineapple juice. Add the maraschino cherries, pineapple, and coconut.
2. Dissolve the sugar in the water and add to the fruit juices.
3. Chill and serve over ice.

Root Beer Fruit Ade

2 teaspoons root beer extract
4 tablespoons sugar or more to sweeten to taste
Juice of lemon, orange, or pineapple
2 quarts (2 l) ice cold water

1. Mix the root beer extract thoroughly with the sugar.
2. Then, and not until then, add the fruit juice and the ice cold water. Stir well and serve.

Chapter 3

Breads

Bread—what home of hard-working people can do without it, even to three times daily? Great variety is possible with a little alteration of foundation recipes. Mastery of good standard recipes for biscuits, muffins, quick loaf bread, plain and fancy yeast bread, will open the door to an endless variety, and establish a firm reputation for good cooking.

Quick breads are mixed and baked quickly. They depend upon baking powder or soda, or a combination of the two, or steam, as leavening agents. Light handling and quick mixing help spell success. That common fault, excess of soda or baking powder, can be avoided if one is familiar with the rules for their use.

Yeast breads take a front place in importance because they do not dry out quickly and have a wide range of uses, as fresh breads, sandwiches, toast, croutons, bread cases. Stale bits of bread and crumbs can be used in many hot dishes and desserts.

Too high a percentage of bread and cereals to other foods is a very possible error in diet and meal planning. The best check is to serve an abundance of milk, vegetables, fruit, and other products of the farm, along with bread of all sorts.

—*The Farmer's Wife*

Quick Breads

Popovers

Makes 8

1 cup (250 ml) flour
¼ teaspoon salt
1 cup (250 ml) milk
2 eggs
1 teaspoon melted butter

1. Heat the oven to 450°F/230°C.
2. Put the flour in a bowl. Make a well in the center and drop in the salt. Add the milk gradually and stir well. When smooth, add the unbeaten eggs and melted butter. Beat until smooth.
3. Fill the greased pans one-third full. Bake in hissing hot muffin pans or hot earthenware or glass cups for about 20–30 minutes. Reduce the heat to 350°F/175°C for about 15 minutes longer or until the popovers are a deep golden brown color. Serve at once.

Note: Popovers, when properly baked, are mostly crisp outer shell and only a little moist material inside. Popovers may be split and filled with dried beef gravy or creamed chicken for a special breakfast or supper dish.

Baking Powder Biscuits

Makes 12–15

2 cups (500 ml) flour
3 teaspoons baking powder
1 teaspoon salt
4 tablespoons shortening
⅔ cup (160 ml) milk

1. Heat the oven to 450°F/230°C.
2. Mix and sift the dry ingredients, work in the shortening quickly with a fork or dough blender.
3. Add the milk all at once and stir lightly to make a soft dough.
4. Turn out on a slightly floured board and knead lightly for a very few seconds. Roll to a ⅓-inch (1-cm) thickness. Cut, dipping the cutter in flour after each using, and transfer to a greased baking sheet. Bake for 10–12 minutes.

Variations

Drop Biscuits: Use 2–3 more tablespoons milk to make the dough of drop consistency. Do not roll out.

Cinnamon Rolls: Roll the dough lightly in an oblong sheet ¼ inch (½ cm) thick, spread with soft butter, sprinkle with a mixture of sugar and cinnamon. Roll up from the long side like a jelly roll. Cut slices ½ inch (1 cm) thick, lay them flat side down on a baking sheet, and bake.

Orange Biscuits: Substitute part orange juice for the milk. On top of each biscuit put a piece of cube sugar that has been soaked in orange juice long enough to absorb some of it but not long enough to dissolve. Grate orange rind over the top.

Shortcake: Increase the shortening to ⅓ cup (80 ml) in the standard recipe or use part cream in place of the milk and mix as for biscuits. Pat out the dough about ¼ inch (½ cm) thick, cut in large rounds for individual shortcakes. Place in pairs before baking, with butter between, or pat out in a thin (to be used double) or a thicker sheet (to be split) in an oblong pan. To serve, place fruit between the layers and on top. Serve with plain cream.

Golden Shortcake: Increase the shortening as for shortcake above to ⅓ cup (80 ml). Add 1 egg, beaten, to ½ cup (125 ml) milk and use as the liquid in place of the plain milk. Bake in muffin tins. Split to serve.

Scotch Scones: Proceed as for the regular biscuits, adding 2 teaspoons sugar to the dry ingredients. In place of the plain milk use ⅓ cup (80 ml) half-and-half mixed with 2 beaten eggs, reserving a little egg white. Roll out and cut in triangles, brush with the egg white, sprinkle with sugar, and bake at 450°F/ 230°C for 12–15 minutes. For raisin scones, add ½ cup (125 ml) raisins.

Sour Milk Griddle Cakes

2 cups (500 ml) flour
2 tablespoons cornmeal
1 teaspoon salt
1 teaspoon baking soda
1–2 tablespoons sugar
2–2⅓ cups (500–575 ml) sour milk or buttermilk
1 egg, beaten
1–3 tablespoons melted butter

1. Mix and sift together the dry ingredients.
2. Add the sour milk, egg, and melted butter, which has been cooled slightly. (If the cakes are baked on a greased griddle, use 1 tablespoon butter.) Beat the batter.
3. Bake the cakes on a hot griddle.

Note: The larger amount of milk is sometimes necessary, if the batter is quite thick. The small amount of cornmeal is not detected but helps give a lighter cake.

Waffles

2 cups (500 ml) flour
½ teaspoon salt
2 teaspoons baking powder
2 tablespoons sugar or honey
2 eggs, well beaten
1½ cups (375 ml) milk
3–6 tablespoons melted butter

1. Mix and sift the dry ingredients.
2. Combine the eggs, milk, and butter and beat. (Use the smaller amount of butter with a greased griddle; the larger amount with an electric iron.) Add to the dry ingredients and beat.
3. Bake in a hot, well-greased waffle iron.

Muffins

Makes 12

2 cups (500 ml) flour
2 teaspoons baking powder
1 teaspoon salt
2 tablespoons sugar
1 egg, beaten
1 cup (250 ml) milk
2 tablespoons melted shortening

1. Heat the oven to 400°F/205°C.
2. Mix and sift the dry ingredients.
3. Combine the liquids (shortening cooled slightly) and pour all at once into the dry ingredients. Stir vigorously until the dry ingredients are just dampened. The batter should not be entirely smooth.
4. Fill the greased tins two-thirds full, with as little extra stirring as possible. Bake for 20–25 minutes. If using cast-iron muffin tins, grease and heat them thoroughly before pouring the batter into them.

Variations

With Sour Milk: Decrease the amount of baking powder to 1 teaspoon. Mix ½ teaspoon baking soda with 1 tablespoon water and add to the wet ingredients. A little more milk may be needed if the batter is quite thick.

With Sour Cream: Use sour cream in place of the milk and omit the shortening. Follow the directions above for sour milk.

Blueberry Muffins: Increase the sugar to ¼ cup (60 ml). Add ⅔ cup (160 ml) fresh berries last. If canned or frozen berries are used, drain well and add to the batter last.

Cranberry Muffins: Use double the amount of shortening and sugar. Add ½ cup (125 ml) raw cranberries cut in halves and 1 additional teaspoon baking powder to the dry ingredients.

Tricks *with* Muffins That Save Time *and* Texture

May 1934

I am willing to make a wager that in almost any group of farm women, the regular biscuit makers will outnumber the regular muffin makers two to one.

Why? Do muffins seem like too much work?

Do they turn out wrong with queer peaks and long tunnels?

There are many meals of course, when biscuits are just the thing, but many times, too, muffins would be a happy choice.

Muffins should be stirred up in a hurry—it is a one, two, three, and then pop them into the oven.

1. Mix together all the dry ingredients.

2. Mix together all the wet ingredients.

3. Combine the two mixtures.

Of course if you want a dress-up muffin, you mix them as you do a cake: cream the fat and sugar, etc. But when you want a quick bread, do it as directed above and you'll have light, delicious muffins ready in a flash.

In fact, the biggest single fault of muffin makers is that they over-mix. Stir just until dry ingredients are dampened, but not smooth or free from lumps, and then stop. Studies at the University of Chicago showed that on the average 20 seconds of mixing gave the best results.

Try this experiment yourself some day when you feel venturesome: measure and mix according to the recipe given for plain muffins, and when ingredients are just dampened nicely and still lumpy, take out batter to fill four or six tins. Then stir what is left a few seconds longer, take out batter for two more; stir some more, and fill another row. Bake them all together and see for yourself how many stirs you should give to secure an even texture. Round tops usually go with even texture and peaked tops with tunnels.

Boston Brown Bread

3 cups (750 ml) coarse flour (1 cup/250 ml rye, 1 cup/250 ml graham, 1 cup/250 ml cornmeal)
1½ teaspoons baking soda
1 teaspoon salt
1 cup (250 ml) raisins
1 egg, beaten
2 cups (500 ml) sour milk
¾ cup (185 ml) molasses

1. Mix and sift the dry ingredients. Add the raisins.
2. Combine the egg, milk, and molasses and add to the dry ingredients. Beat well.
3. Fill 3 greased 1-pound (½-kg) coffee cans or 2 greased 1-quart (1-l) molds two-thirds full and cover. Grease and tie the lids. Steam for 3 hours. Take the cans from the water, uncover, and bake for 30 minutes in the oven to dry.

Notes: To Steam Boston Brown Bread: Place the filled cans or molds on a rack in a deep kettle. Add boiling water to come halfway up around the cans. Cover. Set over heat and steam. Keep the water boiling and add more boiling water as needed to keep the water at the proper level.

With a pressure cooker, steam for 1 hour in 2 inches of water with the petcock open until the bread rises. Finish cooking for 15 minutes at 15 pounds pressure.

Peanut Butter Bread

Makes 1 loaf

2 cups (500 ml) whole wheat flour
1 teaspoon salt
½ teaspoon baking soda
2 teaspoons baking powder
½ cup (125 ml) peanut butter
1 cup (250 ml) sour milk
1 egg, beaten

1. Mix and sift the dry ingredients.
2. Work in the peanut butter.
3. Add the egg to the milk and combine the mixtures to make a thick batter.
4. Grease the coffee cans well and fill two-thirds full. Let stand for 15 minutes.
5. Heat the oven to 325°F/160°C. Bake for 45–50 minutes.

Corn Bread

1 cup (250 ml) cornmeal
1 cup (250 ml) flour
1 teaspoon sugar
1 teaspoon baking soda
1 egg, beaten
1 ⅔ cups (400 ml) sour milk
2 tablespoons melted butter

1. Heat the oven to 425°F/220°C.
2. Mix and sift the dry ingredients.
3. In a separate bowl, mix the egg with the milk and butter.
4. Combine the wet ingredients with the dry.
5. Bake in a greased pan for 30–35 minutes.

Variation

Bacon Corn Bread: Add 1 tablespoon melted bacon fat in place of the melted butter. Sprinkle the top with partially cooked bacon strips before baking.

Spoon Bread

2 cups (500 ml) milk, hot
1 cup (250 ml) cornmeal
4 eggs
4 tablespoons sugar
2 teaspoons baking powder
1 teaspoon salt
2 tablespoons melted shortening

1. Heat the oven to 350°F/175°C.
2. Heat the milk and pour over the cornmeal in a mixing bowl.
3. Beat the eggs and combine with the sugar, then add the mixture to the milk and cornmeal.
4. Stir in the baking powder, salt, and shortening, and beat. It is a very thin batter.
5. Bake at once in a round glass, aluminum, or graniteware baking pan for about 40 minutes. If the baking pan is heavy, preheat it slightly. Serve with a spoon from the pan in which it was baked. This bread has a custardlike consistency.

Quick Nut Bread

Makes 2 loaves

2 cups (500 ml) white flour
1 teaspoon salt
4 teaspoons baking powder
2 cups (500 ml) whole wheat flour
1 cup (250 ml) brown sugar
1 cup (250 ml) chopped nuts
2 eggs, beaten
2 cups (500 ml) milk
2 tablespoons melted butter

1. Heat the oven to 350°F/175°C.
2. Mix and sift the flour, salt, and baking powder. Add the whole wheat flour, sugar, and nuts.
3. In a separate bowl, combine the eggs, milk, and butter.
4. Combine the wet and dry ingredients and pour into two greased bread tins. Let stand for 15–20 minutes. Bake for 50–60 minutes.

Maple Syrup Graham Bread

Makes 2 loaves

2 cups (500 ml) all-purpose flour
2 teaspoons baking powder
2 teaspoons baking soda
1 teaspoon salt
2 cups (500 ml) graham flour
2 eggs
1½ cups (375 ml) buttermilk
½ cup (125 ml) sour cream
1⅓ cups maple syrup

1. Heat the oven to 325°F/160°C.
2. Blend the flour, baking powder, baking soda, and salt. Stir in the graham flour.
3. In a separate bowl, beat the eggs and blend in the buttermilk, sour cream, and maple syrup.
4. Pour the liquid mixture into the dry ingredients and stir well.
5. Grease two medium-size loaf pans, line with waxed paper, and grease again. (Syrup will stick to the sides of the pans, if the pans are not prepared in this manner.) Pour the batter into the pans. Bake until a wooden toothpick inserted into the center of the loaf comes out dry, approximately 1 hour.

Baking Insurance

July 1932

Accurate measuring cups and spoons and knowing how to handle them provide the best good baking insurance a woman can have. With this equipment and knowledge, she can follow tested recipes and get at least reasonably satisfactory results rather than a failure as of old when she tried her neighbor's recipe and used her own cup. Why? In times past her idea and her neighbor's idea of cups and spoonfuls were not the same—while today we have a common standard.

The common standard measuring cup is one approved by the U.S. Bureau of Standards, which contains 8 fluid ounces, or ½ pint, and has the subdivisions of fourths and thirds marked on it. The tablespoon holds ¹⁄₁₆ of a cup or 3 teaspoonfuls. A nest of four measuring spoons may be obtained, ranging from ¼ teaspoon to 1 tablespoon, and what work it saves!

After getting the proper equipment with which to measure, the important thing to remember is that all measurements are level. That old expression of heaping tablespoon has been the Waterloo of more than one cook, so beware! To get level measurements slightly different methods must be used for different ingredients.

Measuring Flour

For instance, flour must be sifted before measuring, otherwise through packing there may be a difference of between a quarter to a half a cup. Then in order to keep it unpacked, a spoon should be used to lift the flour gently into the measuring cup from which it is leveled by using the sharp edge of a spatula or knife.

Measuring Liquids

When a recipe calls for 2 tablespoonfuls of liquid, such as milk or water, that means brimming full; the spoon should be dipped into the liquid to get it this way. When a cupful is being measured, have the cup setting level on a table, for as you know, too much liquid or too little can make a great difference in the finished product.

Measuring Shortening

Shortening can be measured accurately several ways. For instance, butter: 2 cups = 1 pound (½ kg). If your recipe calls for a half cup of butter, a quarter of a pound mold would be the right amount.

For less than a cupful, many people find it easier to measure by spoonfuls, packing the shortening firmly and leveling it off with the sharp edge of a knife. In this case, one might prefer to measure by the displacement method, by filling the measuring cup half full of water, then adding shortening until the water fills the cup. The water is then poured off. Another, and some think better, method is to press the shortening firmly into the measuring cup up to the mark of the amount needed.

Measuring Brown Sugar

Brown sugar, as well as shortening, should be pressed in tightly to measure accurately and leveled off on top, while granulated sugar may be measured by filling the cup directly and leveling off.

Measuring Baking Powder

Leavening agents, such as baking powder, should be measured with the ut-most precision, since a little less or a little more affects the finished product to a great extent.

There are three different types of baking powder named according to the acid reacting substance in them. They are known as tartrate (tartaric acid, cream of tartar), phosphate (calcium or sodium add phosphate), and combination or S.A.S. Phosphate (sodium aluminum sulfate).

Special proportions have been worked out by the manufacturers of each, which makes for the most perfect product. Therefore, it is well to read the label carefully on your own baking powder can and use the proportions suggested in your recipe. Do not measure off from the rounded sides of the baking powder can, but dip the measuring spoon in to fill it, then level off with a sharp edge of a knife, or the special straight-edge leveling device found in some new cans.

Yeast Breads

Important Things to Remember in Baking Bread

Temperature of Sponge and Dough: Between 80°F/27°C and 85°F/29°C is best. In cold weather, when the room and flour are cool, use warmer water. To keep the dough warm, set the dough in a closed cupboard with a bowl of hot water. In summer, cool liquids more than usual so that the sponge is not too warm.
Kneading: This helps develop the gluten. Knead with a light, springy motion, using the heel of the palm, near the wrist. Curve the fingers to keep the dough round and full.
Making into Loaves: Shape, using little or no flour. Allow the dough to stand a few minutes between cutting for loaves.
Baking: A well-baked loaf is brown all over with the bottom and sides lighter than the top, a crisp, even crust, and an even texture throughout.

White Bread

Makes 2 loaves

1 package (2¾ teaspoons) dry yeast
¼ cup (60 ml) warm water
2 tablespoons sugar
3 tablespoons melted butter or shortening
2 cups (500 ml) warm milk
6 cups all-purpose flour
1 tablespoon salt

1. In a large mixing bowl, dissolve the yeast in the water and let stand for 10 minutes.
2. Add the sugar, shortening, warm milk, and half the flour or enough flour to make a batter. Beat until smooth. Add the salt and remaining flour, to make a dough that can be handled. Knead for 10–15 minutes.

3. Place the dough in a greased bowl, cover, and let rise at a temperature of 80°–85°F/27°–29°C until doubled in volume, approximately 1½ hours.

5. Knead down slightly without using more flour and let rise again.

6. Divide and shape the dough into 2 loaves. Place in well-greased, medium-size loaf pans. Cover, return to a warm place, and let rise until double.

7. Heat the oven to 425°F/220°C and bake for 15 minutes. Reduce the heat to 375°F/190°C and finish baking, approximately 35–45 minutes.

Dinner Rolls

Makes 24 rolls

2 packages (5½ teaspoons) dry yeast
¼ cup (60 ml) warm water
1 egg
¼ cup (60 ml) sugar
½ cup (125 ml) mashed potato
½ cup (125 ml) milk
⅓ cup (80 ml) butter
½ teaspoon salt
3–3½ cups (750–875 ml) all-purpose flour

1. Dissolve the yeast in the warm water and set aside.

2. In a large bowl, blend the egg and sugar. Add the potato, milk, butter, salt, and yeast mixture. Beat for 1 minute.

3. Stir in the flour ½ cup (125 ml) at a time. When the dough becomes firm, work in the remaining flour by hand until it loses its stickiness.

4. Turn the dough onto a floured surface and knead until it becomes smooth, approximately 10 minutes. Grease the bowl; put the dough in, cover, and let rise in a warm spot until double in volume, approximately 1½ hours.

5. Divide the dough in half. On a floured surface, roll the dough by hand into a 12-inch rope. Cut into 12 pieces and shape each piece into a ball. Arrange in an 8- or 9-inch (20- or 22.5-cm) cake pan. Brush tops of dough with melted butter, cover, and let rise in warm spot until double in size.

6. Heat the oven to 400°F/205°C. Bake for 13–16 minutes or until golden brown. Place on rack to cool and brush immediately with melted butter.

Oatmeal Bread

Makes 2 loaves

2 packages (5½ teaspoons) dry yeast
½ cup (125 ml) warm water
1¼ cups (300 ml) warm milk
¼ cup (60 ml) firmly packed brown sugar
1 tablespoon salt
3 tablespoons butter
5–6 cups (1250–1500 ml) all-purpose flour
1 cup (250 ml) quick rolled oats
1 tablespoon oil

1. Dissolve the yeast in the warm water.
2. Add the milk, sugar, salt, and butter.
3. Add 2 cups (500 ml) flour and beat until smooth, approximately 3 minutes, by hand. Add 1 cup (250 ml) flour and the rolled oats. Beat until smooth, about 150 strokes. Add enough flour to make a soft dough.
4. Turn onto a floured surface and knead for 8–10 minutes or until smooth and elastic. Cover and allow the dough to rest for 20 minutes.
5. Divide the dough in half. Roll each half into a 12x8-inch (30x20-cm) rectangle and shape into loaves. Place each loaf into a greased, medium-size loaf pan and brush with oil. Cover and refrigerate the dough overnight.
6. When ready to bake, remove from the refrigerator and let stand uncovered for 20 minutes at room temperature. Heat the oven to 400°F/205°C and bake for 35–40 minutes or until done.

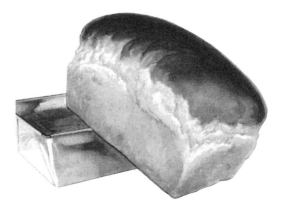

Swedish Limpa Rye Bread

Makes 2 loaves

3 cups (750 ml) all-purpose flour
2½ cups (625 ml) rye flour
¼ cup (60 ml) sugar
1 tablespoon salt
2 packages (5½ teaspoons) dry yeast
1½ cups (375 ml) milk
½ cup (125 ml) water
2 tablespoons molasses
2 tablespoons butter
1 cup (250 ml) raisins, chopped
2 tablespoons grated orange peel
1 tablespoon oil

1. Combine the flours in one bowl.
2. In a separate, larger bowl, thoroughly mix 2 cups (500 ml) flour mixture with the sugar, salt, and undissolved yeast. Reserve the remaining 3½ cups flour mixture.
3. Combine the milk, water, molasses, and butter in saucepan. Heat until very warm.
4. Gradually add the wet ingredients to the mixture of flours, sugar, salt, and yeast. Beat for 5 minutes by hand. Add ¾ cup (185 ml) reserve flour mixture and beat for 5 minutes. Stir in the raisins, orange peel, and enough reserve flour mixture until the dough is stiff.
5. Turn out onto a floured surface and knead about 10 minutes or until smooth and elastic. If necessary, add additional all-purpose flour to obtain the desired dough. Cover and let rest for 30 minutes.
6. Divide the dough in half and form each half into a smooth ball. Flatten each ball into a mound about 7 inches in diameter. Place each mound in a greased 8-inch pan or on a greased baking sheet. Brush the loaves with oil. Cover and refrigerate overnight.
7. When ready to bake, remove from the refrigerator and let stand uncovered for 20 minutes at room temperature. Meanwhile, heat oven to 375°F/190°C. Bake for 35–40 minutes or until done. Remove from the pans or sheet and cool on wire racks. If desired, brush with melted butter immediately.

For Home Bakers

by Mabel K. Ray, March 1932

Bread "like Mother used to make" is once more appearing on many a table, much to the delight of the family. For mother cannot only make mighty good bread, but can make Parker House rolls, pecan rolls, Dutch apple cake, and many other appetizing varieties from the same ordinary, plain bread dough.

What are the secrets of making good bread, and how can we make some of these other good things?

Secrets of Making Good Bread

In making bread, one may use the straight dough or the sponge method with equally good results. With straight dough, the materials are all mixed together from the beginning, while with the sponge, part of the flour and the shortening are added after the first rising.

When using dry yeast, a little more should be allowed since the yeast plants are in a less active state than in the compressed and need more time to grow. Thus the overnight sponge is especially good to use with the dry yeast. Get the sponge in a spot where the temperature is 60–70°F/15–20°C if you are using the overnight process, or 80–82°F/26–27°C if you are using the short one.

Sugar is added to give the yeast plants an easily obtained food, and also for flavor and a brown tender crust. Moisture in the air is needed to help keep the top of the dough from developing a hard crust, and is often supplied by setting it over a pan of warm water. Cover the sponge and dough lightly with a cloth to prevent excess evaporation.

Salt is added to help the flavor but mostly to regulate the growth of the yeast and fermentation. It keeps fermentation from taking place too rapidly if added in the right proportion, but if an oversupply is used, the process is slowed up too much and a heavy bread is produced. Therefore, measure accurately the amount given in your recipe.

Shortening helps give a tenderness, flakiness, and palatability, and increases the length of time the bread will stay fresh.

The flour to make good bread must be of the right type, gluten content, purity, and temperature. There are two types: hard wheat and soft wheat flour. The former is the best for bread baking since it is much richer in gluten, a protein which is elastic when moistened. The elasticity of the gluten makes it possible for the gas formed in bread by yeast plants to expand the gluten or cause the dough to rise.

Hard wheat flour may be distinguished from soft by its gritty feel and the fact that it falls apart loosely when handled. If soft wheat flour is used in making bread, more will be needed than if the hard is used.

The temperature of the flour and water have much to do with the action of yeast plants. The ordinary room temperature is best. Sift flour several times before using to warm it, add air, and make possible more accurate measurement.

The water or milk added to make bread should be warm but never over 110°F/45°C, or the yeast plants will be killed. An average temperature of the flour, liquid, and room should be 80–82°F/26–27°C to obtain the best results.

Menu: The Ideal Loaf

And what are the best results in a loaf of bread? The ideal loaf is attractive in appearance and well rounded on top; it is light for its size, and has a smooth, tender, brown, unbroken, crisp crust. The crumb should be spongy and tender, slightly moist and have no dark streaks, and the texture should be fine and even. The bread should smell good and have a delicious nutty flavor.

Problems with Bread

Possibly you have had a poorly shaped, bulging loaf with a broken crust. This may have been caused by too much dough in the pan, too long a rising, inexperience in molding a loaf, cooling too fast, or baking in either an overly hot or an overly slow oven.

Streaked bread, which everyone detests, is generally due to mixing poorly or to using poor flour, although overfermentation, stale yeast, or too cool an oven have a tendency to cause the same thing.

For that sour unpleasant odor that sometimes accompanies bread, it is well to check up on the quality of the yeast and flour and to find out whether the bread was permitted to rise too long and in too hot a room.

If the crumb of your bread is heavy, crumbly, and dry, too stiff a dough was mixed, there was not enough yeast to cause it to rise sufficiently, or it was baked too long at too low a temperature.

A coarse and uneven texture is another difficulty which we often have. It may be due to overfermentation, not enough flour, or too cool an oven to start with.

A thick tough crust is caused by a lack of shortening and baking in an oven with too dry a heat.

Sweet Rolls

2 packages (5½ teaspoons) dry yeast
½ cup (125 ml) warm water
½ cup (125 ml) milk, scalded and cooled
½ cup (125 ml) sugar
1 teaspoon salt
2 eggs, beaten
½ cup (125 ml) butter or shortening
5 cups (1250 ml) all-purpose flour

1. Dissolve the yeast in the warm water.
2. Stir in the milk, sugar, salt, eggs, and butter.
3. Add half the flour and beat until smooth. Mix in enough remaining flour to make the dough easy to handle.
4. Turn out onto a floured surface and knead until smooth, about 10 minutes. Place in a greased bowl, turn so all surfaces are greased. Cover and let rise in a warm spot until doubled in volume, approximately 1½ hours.
5. Shape as desired, place in greased baking tins or on sheets, and let rise until double in bulk.
6. Heat the oven to 375°F/190°C and bake for 25–30 minutes.

Variations

Cinnamon Rolls: Roll out the dough in a narrow, long sheet. Spread generously with butter. Sprinkle with brown sugar, cinnamon, and whole raisins. Roll so that the whole roll has only 2 or 3 turnings. Cut and place the rolls in a pan (grease the sides) with butter and brown sugar in the bottom. Sprinkle the top of each roll with sugar and cinnamon.

Coffee Cake: Add raisins to the dough and roll out a piece to fit a fairly shallow pan. Cover and let rise to double bulk. Before baking, brush with beaten egg and cover with a mixture of 3 tablespoons softened butter, ½ cup (125 ml) sugar, and 1 teaspoon cinnamon.

Chapter 4

Meats

The term "meat" applies to flesh food, including beef, pork, and mutton, and in a general way, includes fish and poultry. Meat deserves a place in our meals once or twice daily. The usual rule is to have two servings of protein food each day. The protein group of foods includes meat substitutes such as eggs, cheese, and dried beans, besides meat.

Even though a family does its own butchering and has an abundant supply of meat, moderation is wise. To continually overeat may result in strain and injury to digestive systems. But from the standpoint of both food value and flavor, well-planned meals will frequently include meat, either as the main dish or in combination with other foods.
—*The Farmer's Wife*

Beef and Veal

Frying Tender Steaks or Chops

1. Sear the steak quickly on both sides in a hot skillet that is slightly greased. Then cook more slowly, turning occasionally. Do not cover and do not add any water. If extra grease forms, pour it off.

2. A thick steak can be first seared, then put in a hot oven on a rack in a dripping pan to cook to the desired stage.

3. Pork is always cooked well done; beef and lamb, from rare to well done. Transfer to a hot platter. Serve at once.

Frying Less Tender Steaks or Chops

1. Pound the steaks or chops well until quite thin, adding flour and seasonings.

2. Sear in hot fat and then cook more slowly until done. The pounding may be enough to make it tender.

3. Some steaks will be improved if a little water is added and the skillet covered for several minutes over a slow heat.

Roasting a Tender Cut

1. Wipe the meat with a damp cloth; trim or tie in the shape needed. Rub the outside lightly with seasoned flour. Place on the oven rack, uncovered, in an open roaster or dripping pan with the fat side up. If necessary, lay strips of fat meat or bacon on top, or baste with melted fat.

2. Roast at 450°F/230°C for 20–30 minutes to brown. Finish roasting, still uncovered, at 300°F/150°C until done, allowing 20–25 minutes per pound of meat for a medium-done roast.

3. If it is not convenient to start the roast in a hot oven and then reduce the heat quickly, a satisfactory roast can be secured by starting in a slow to moderate oven. Increase the heat and brown the roast at the end. There is much less shrinkage and waste if most of the roasting is done slowly.

4. Rib roasts of beef, leg and shoulder of lamb, fresh shoulder and ham of pork, tender cured ham, and young poultry are all suited to this method of roasting.

Roasting a Less Tender Cut

1. Prepare the meat as for a tender roast, rubbing the outside with seasoned flour, then searing in a hot oven or in a heavy kettle.
2. When brown on all sides, place the meat on the oven rack, and add from ½–1 cup (125–250 ml) of water. Cook until tender in either a covered roaster in the oven or in a heavy covered kettle on top of the stove.
3. Vegetables can be added during the last hour of cooking. Pot roasts, chuck roasts, less tender steaks, and older poultry are suited to this method of roasting.

Boiled Dinner

Serves 4–6

4 pounds (2 kg) corned beef
6 carrots, cut in lengthwise pieces
6 slices of turnip
4 onions, parboil if strong
6–8 potatoes, quartered
1 small head cabbage, quartered

1. Cover the meat with cold water and bring slowly to the boiling point. Boil for 5 minutes and remove any scum. Cover and simmer until tender, about 30 minutes to each pound of meat.
2. A half hour before the meat is done, add the carrots, turnips, onions, and potatoes; 15 minutes later, add the cut-up cabbage.
3. To serve, arrange the meat in the center of a large platter. Group the vegetables around the meat.

Swiss Steak

Serves 4–6

3 pounds (1½ kg) round steak, 1 inch (2½ cm) thick
1–1½ cups (250–375 ml) flour
2 teaspoons salt
2 tablespoons oil, divided
2 medium onions, sliced
2 medium carrots, diced
½ green pepper, diced
6 cups (1500 ml) tomatoes

1. Heat the oven to 350°F/175°C.
2. Trim the steak and cut into large servings. Pound the flour and salt into the meat. (Thorough pounding will help make the meat more tender and shorten the baking time.)
3. Brown the steak well in the oil in a hot, lightly greased frying pan and place in a casserole or skillet with a tight cover.
4. Brown the onions, carrots, and green pepper slightly in the oil. Add the tomatoes. Stir until the liquid has absorbed the rich brown from the bottom of the skillet.
5. Pour the vegetables and their liquid over the meat. Bake for 2½–3 hours, and serve.

Variation

Sour Cream Steak: Omit the carrots, green pepper, and tomatoes from the Swiss Steak. Brown the onions, put on top of the meat, and add 1 cup (250 ml) boiling water. Cover and cook until the water is nearly absorbed. Add 1–1½ cups (250–375 ml) sour cream and finish baking until tender. Make a thinner gravy, if desired, by adding water or milk to the pan gravy.

Veal Cutlets
En Casserole

Serves 4–6

2 pounds (1 kg) veal
¼ cup (60 ml) oil
2 tablespoons flour
½ teaspoon salt
¼ teaspoon pepper
¼ teaspoon paprika
2–3 tablespoons water
1 cup (250 ml) sour cream
1 tablespoon onion juice
1 cup (250 ml) chopped mushrooms, if desired

1. Heat the oven to 350°F/175°C.
2. Cut the veal in pieces 2 inches (5 cm) square and brown quickly in the hot oil. Place in a casserole.
3. Make a smooth paste of the flour and seasonings mixed with a little water. Stir in the sour cream. Cook until slightly thickened. Add the onion juice and mushrooms.
4. Pour the sauce over the meat. Cover the casserole and bake for 1 hour, and serve.

City Chicken

Serves 4–6

1½ pounds (¾ kg) fresh veal
1½ pounds (¾ kg) boneless pork
10 skewers
Flour
Salt and pepper
2 eggs, beaten
Bread crumbs
2–4 tablespoons oil
1 cup (250 ml) water

1. Heat the oven to 350°F/175°C.
2. Cut the veal and pork into ½-inch (1-cm) squares. Place alternately on skewers until they are two-thirds filled. Roll in the flour seasoned with the salt and pepper; then the beaten eggs; then the bread crumbs.
3. Heat a small amount of oil in a frying pan and brown the skewers of meat on all sides. Put in a roaster and add 1 cup (250 ml) water. Cover and roast until tender, about 1 hour, and serve.

Let's Have Meat

by Mabel K. Ray

Tsizz

What meat will we have for dinner? How shall it be prepared? What shall we serve with it? These are questions to be answered daily in nearly every household. But they are not difficult questions since there is a wide choice in kinds and cuts of meat, and enough ways to prepare them to have meat served a different way each of the three hundred and sixty-five days of the year.

Cooking Temperatures

Even though only the simple standby methods of meat cookery such as roasting are used, there are new pointers to learn from experimental work being done on meat. It has been found that in general meats are not so dry, the juices are kept to a greater extent, and there is less shrinkage if low and medium temperatures of heat are used in cooking rather than high.

Is this meant for cured meats as well? Yes.

"For cured pork, as for fresh pork," according to the U.S. Department of Agriculture, "thorough cooking at slow to moderate temperatures is the secret of success, whether the meat is fried, broiled, roasted, steamed, or cooked in water." Twenty-five to thirty minutes per pound is usually needed to bake hams well done. All pork should be cooked well done to guard against trichinosis, a disease caused by an organism often occurring in raw pork.

There's also a trick to making bacon that delicious, crispy, golden brown. Put a layer of bacon in a cool frying pan and cook slowly over a low fire until the desired crispness is reached and the bacon is a light golden brown. Bacon should be turned frequently while cooking, and the surplus fat poured off as it fries out.

Searing

Do you sear your roasts and chops? Why? The reason usually given is to reduce shrinkage and loss of juices. But this will have to be changed, since experiments have proved that searing increases the cooking losses, and that it does not always make certain that juices will be retained. Most people, however, prefer to sear their chops and some their roasts, due to the flavor it gives. But after searing, finish the cooking at low or medium temperature.

Roasting

Excellent roasts can be prepared without searing by cooking at a low or medium temperature throughout the process. The open pan seems to have its advantages for roasts other than veal and poultry, due to less moisture loss. Let us remind the inexperienced cook to place roasts with the fat side up so that they can baste themselves.

As to time of salting, it makes little difference in the losses in the meat. Salt, during the cooking process, does not penetrate far but does give a grayer color to the first layer of meat.

Cooks in the past have had to rely solely on judgment gained through years of experience to know when roasts were the right degree of "doneness." But, even with the best of cooks, mistakes were sometimes made—the roasts being too done or too rare, and not "just right." Today even the inexperienced cook may have a perfect roast, thanks to the development of a special meat thermometer. It is placed in the middle of the roast, and when it registers 140°F/ 60°C inner temperature, it is done rare; for a medium done it should register between 140–160°F/60–70°C; and for well done,

between 175–185°F/80–85°C.

Broiling and Pan Broiling

When it comes to broiling or pan broiling cuts of meats it is well to cook one side, turn to the other side, cook that, then serve. Continuous turning dries the meat out too much.

Cooking with Moist Heat

As experienced cooks know, roasting and broiling are methods used for the more tender cuts of meat, while pot roasting, braising, stewing, and soup making are the main ways to utilize the less tender cuts. Grinding the less tender meat, pounding, or cooking with an acid, such as tomatoes, are other aids to gain tenderness. The less tender cuts of meats have a greater amount of connective tissue, and it has been found that cooking with moist heat, brought about by adding water for the cooking process, softens this connective tissue. The tender cuts come from the part of the animal exercised the least and the less tender from the parts exercised a great deal.

Ground Meat

Hamburger Royal

Serves 4–6

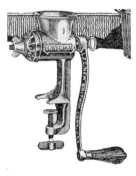

½ small onion, chopped
3 tablespoons butter, divided
1 egg, beaten
½ cup (125 ml) bread crumbs
2 tablespoons catsup
Milk to moisten
Salt and pepper
1 pound (½ kg) lean ground beef
1 cup (250 ml) chopped mushrooms
Parsley for garnish

1. Brown the onion in 1 tablespoon butter.
2. Add the onion and the other ingredients (except the mushrooms) to the ground meat and blend.
3. Shape into one flat steak or individual cakes. Cook in an uncovered, lightly greased skillet slowly until done.
4. Brown the mushrooms in 2 tablespoons butter. Make a gravy from the juice in the pan and add the mushrooms. Place the meat on a platter and pour the mushroom gravy around it. Garnish with the parsley and serve.

Baby Porcupines

Serves 4–6

1 pound (½ kg) ground round steak
1 cup (250 ml) bread crumbs
1 egg
4 tablespoons chopped onion
Salt and pepper
¼ cup (60 ml) raw rice
1 can tomato soup, 10¾ ounces (305 g)
2 cups (500 ml) boiling water

1. Mix the meat, bread crumbs, egg, chopped onion, salt, and pepper.
2. Shape into round oblong cakes and roll in the uncooked rice.
3. Heat the tomato soup and water in a Dutch oven. Place the cakes in this mixture and cover. Bring to a simmer and cook about 1 hour, and serve.

Swedish Kol Dolma

Serves 4–6

1 pound (½ kg) ground beef or veal
1 pound (½ kg) ground pork
1 cup (250 ml) raw rice
1 tablespoon salt
1 tablespoon sugar
⅓ teaspoon pepper
⅓ teaspoon nutmeg
2 eggs, beaten
Large cabbage leaves
Drippings
1½ cups (375 ml) water

1. Mix together the beef, pork, rice, and seasonings. Add the beaten eggs.
2. Place the large cabbage leaves in boiling, salted water until just softened. Drain gently.
3. Place 2 tablespoons of the meat mixture in each leaf and wrap well. Place in a Dutch oven or heavy roaster with the drippings and 1½ cups (375 ml) water. Cover, bring to simmer, and cook for 1½–2 hours.

Swedish Meatballs

Serves 4–6

1 pound (½ kg) ground round steak
½ pound (250 g) ground pork steak
1 medium potato, mashed
½ cup (125 ml) bread crumbs
1 egg yolk
Hot milk
1 teaspoon sugar
Salt and pepper
Pinch of ginger
Grating of nutmeg
Flour
½ pint half-and-half or cream

1. Heat the oven to 350°F/175°C.
2. Mix the meat, mashed potato, bread crumbs, egg yolk, and a small amount of hot milk to make soft. Season with the sugar, salt, pepper, ginger, and nutmeg.
3. Form the meat mixture into small balls, roll in the flour, and brown in a frying pan with a small amount of oil. Bake for 15–20 minutes. Pour the cream over the top of the meat and continue to cook until brown.

Pork

Baked Stuffed Pork Shoulder

Serves 4–6

5- to 7-pound (2¼- to 3-kg) pork shoulder
Salt and pepper
Poultry dressing
Flour

1. Heat the oven to 450°F/230°C.
2. Trim the shoulder and remove the bones, leaving a pocket in the meat. Sew up the small opening, leaving one corner open where the shoulder blade was removed.
3. Sprinkle the meat inside with the salt and pepper, and pile in a light, well-seasoned dressing. Sew up the sides. Rub with the flour and more salt and pepper.
4. Place on a rack in an open roaster and place in the oven. When slightly brown and sizzling, reduce the heat to 350°F/175°C. Roast until well done, allowing 25–30 minutes per pound of meat.

Arabian Casserole

Serves 4–6

6 pork chops
Flour
Salt and pepper
2 onions, sliced
½ cup (125 ml) raw rice, washed
2 cups (500 ml) tomatoes
1 cup (250 ml) water

1. Heat the oven to 350°F/175°C.
2. Rub the pork chops with the flour seasoned with the salt and pepper, and brown in a frying pan with a little fat.
3. Place in a casserole or baking dish; top with the sliced onions and a mound of rice.
4. Heat the tomatoes and add to the casserole with the water. Cover and bake for 1 hour or until the rice is tender, basting the rice occasionally with the tomato. Serve from the baking dish.

Pork Chops and Lima Beans

Serves 4–6

1 pound (½ kg) lima beans
½ teaspoon mustard
2 tablespoons sugar
2 tablespoons chopped onion
½ cup (125 ml) tomato catsup
Salt and pepper
1 pound (½ kg) pork chops

1. Heat the oven to 350°F/175°C.
2. Cook the lima beans in enough water to cover until partly tender. Add the mustard, sugar, onion, catsup, and salt to taste. Pour into a large, flat baking dish and add enough more water to cover the beans.
3. Season the chops with the salt and pepper, place on top of the beans, cover, and bake for 1–1½ hours. Uncover at the end of the baking period to brown, and serve.

Stuffed Pork Tenderloin

Serves 4–6

1- to 2-pound (½- to 1-kg) pork tenderloin
Poultry dressing
Pickles
Flour
Salt and pepper

1. Heat the oven to 350°F/175°C.
2. Split a pork tenderloin in half lengthwise, but leave the halves joined together. Pound each half slightly.
3. Fill with the poultry dressing seasoned with a few chopped pickles. The stuffing should be arranged so that it will be higher in the center. Fasten the edges of the meat together and sprinkle with the flour, salt, and pepper.
4. Roast uncovered for about 1 hour, basting occasionally, and serve.

Ham and Sour Cream Casserole

Serves 4–6

2½ cups (625 ml) dried noodles
3 quarts (3 l) water
Salt
1 onion, chopped
2 teaspoons chopped parsley
3 tablespoons butter
1 pound (½ kg) cooked ham, cut into small pieces
3 eggs, beaten
½ teaspoon ground nutmeg
⅛ teaspoon pepper
2 cups (500 ml) sour cream
1 cup (250 ml) bread crumbs

1. Boil the noodles for 10 minutes in the salted water, and drain.
2. Heat the oven to 350°F/175°C.
3. Brown the onion and parsley in the butter. Add the ham, and remove from the stove.
4. Beat together the eggs, nutmeg, pepper, and cream, and add to the ham. Add the drained noodles, and mix.
5. Place in a greased baking dish and spread the bread crumbs on top. Bake uncovered for 30 minutes or until set.

Scrapple

Yields 5–10 pounds

1 pig's head
4 pig's feet and hocks
1 pound (½ kg) pork trimmings
Veal stewing bones
Cornmeal
Salt and pepper
Sage

1. Place the well-cleaned pig's head, feet, hocks, and pork trimmings in a kettle with the veal bones, and cover with water. Cover the kettle and cook until the meat leaves the bones. Lift it with a skimmer to a platter to cool.
2. Let the liquor cook, then remove the grease.
3. Remove all the bones and gristle and cut the meat in small pieces.
4. Return the liquor to the kettle. When boiling, thicken it by adding yellow cornmeal, sifted in slowly through the fingers: 1 cup (250 ml) cornmeal per quart of liquor.

5. Add the meat and season well with the salt, pepper, and powdered sage to taste. Reduce the heat, cover, and cook slowly for 1 hour.

6. Pour into a deep square pan to cool and set. When cold, turn onto a platter, cover, and refrigerate until needed.

To Prepare Scrapple: Cut in slices ½ inch (1 cm) thick and fry; or dip in beaten egg, then in fine bread crumbs or cornmeal, and fry.

Delicious Ham Loaf

Serves 4–6

1½ pounds (¾ kg) ground smoked ham
1½ pounds (¾ kg) lean pork
½ teaspoon salt
¼ teaspoon pepper
1 teaspoon onion juice
½ cup (125 ml) rolled oats
½ cup (125 ml) cracker or bread crumbs
2 eggs, beaten
1¼ cups (300 ml) tomato juice, divided
8 whole cloves

1. Heat the oven to 325°F/160°C.
2. Mix all the ingredients, except the cloves and ¼ cup (60 ml) of the tomato juice. Shape into a loaf and place in a loaf pan.
3. Pour the rest of the tomato juice over the top and stick with the cloves.
4. Bake uncovered for 2–2½ hours. If the loaf pan is set inside a pan of water it will make a moister loaf.

Pork and Veal Loaf

Serves 4–6

2 pounds (1 kg) ground veal
1 pound (½ kg) ground lean pork
1½ teaspoons salt
1 teaspoon pepper
½ teaspoon nutmeg
⅛ teaspoon allspice
1 cup (250 ml) bread crumbs
2 eggs, beaten
1 cup (250 ml) milk

1. Heat the oven to 350°F/175°C.
2. Mix all the ingredients and shape in a loaf pan.
3. Bake for 2 hours, and serve.

Sauces for Meats and Vegetables

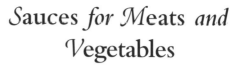

It's the sauce that gives many a dish distinction, that lifts it up from the ordinary. Once a person is master of the rules for making two or three basic sauces, she can vary vegetables, meat, desserts, and other dishes endlessly. Remember that the sauce or accompaniment is like the right accessory to a dress. Certain flavors belong.

A sauce should add contrast in flavor and usually contrast in color, as a white or yellow egg sauce with salmon loaf or a chocolate sauce with vanilla ice cream. When a main dish or dessert is to be served at the table, you may reserve part of the sauce in a separate bowl to be added to each serving or passed for each person to use as desired.

| White Sauces | | | | |
Sauce	Butter	Flour	Milk	Salt
Thin	1 tablespoon	1 tablespoon	1 cup (250 ml)	½ teaspoon
Medium	2 tablespoons	2 tablespoons	1 cup (250 ml)	½ teaspoon
Thick	3 tablespoons	3–4 tablespoons	1 cup (250 ml)	½ teaspoon

A double boiler is helpful in making a smooth sauce. Melt the butter. Add the flour and blend. Add the milk and stir until thickened. The milk may be heated until scalding and a part of it added first, then the rest, keeping the sauce smooth as you stir.

Variations

These variations are based on 1 cup (250 ml) medium white sauce:

Carrot Golden Sauce: Add 2 tablespoons minced, cooked carrot or ¼ cup (60 ml) finely shredded raw carrot.

Cheese Sauce: Add ½ cup (125 ml) American cheese cut in small pieces.

Cream Sauce: Substitute part cream for the milk.

East India Sauce: Add ½–1 teaspoon curry powder.

Egg Sauce: Add 1 or 2 diced hard-boiled eggs.

Lobster, Shrimp, And Oyster Sauce: Add ¼ cup (60 ml) meat, minced finely, to the cream sauce. Use for timbales, vegetable loaf, etc.

Paprika Sauce: Add 1–2 teaspoons paprika. Use for white vegetables such as cabbage and onion.

Parsley Sauce: Add 2 tablespoons finely chopped parsley to either an egg or plain sauce.

Pimento Sauce: Add 2 tablespoons chopped pimento, or red and green sweet pepper, mixed.

Tomato Sauce: Substitute strained tomatoes for the milk and season with onion juice, or scraped onion, cayenne, or black pepper.

Quick Mushroom Cream Sauce
Ingredients
1 can condensed mushroom soup, 10¾ ounces (305 g)
1 egg yolk, beaten
½ cup (125 ml) milk

Heat the soup in a saucepan. Add the egg yolk and milk. Stir until thickened.

Spanish Sauce
Ingredients
2 tablespoons butter
2 tablespoons chopped celery
2 tablespoons chopped onion
1½ cups (375 ml) tomatoes
1 tablespoon sugar
½ teaspoon salt
2 tablespoons flour
2 tablespoons vinegar

1. Melt the butter and brown the celery and onion in a heavy saucepan or skillet. Add the tomatoes and cook 5 minutes.
2. Mix the dry ingredients. Blend with the vinegar and add to the first mixture. Cook until thickened, stirring continually.

Grape Juice Sauce
Ingredients
1 tablespoon cornstarch
2 tablespoons cold water
¼ cup (60 ml) hot water
1 cup (250 ml) grape juice
Juice of 1 lemon

1. In a heavy saucepan, mix the cornstarch with the cold water and add the hot water.
2. Cook until the mixture thickens. Add the fruit juices. Serve hot, especially good with ham, tongue, or duck.

Brown Sauce
Ingredients
2 tablespoons minced onion
1 tablespoon minced sweet pepper
3 tablespoons butter
5 tablespoons flour
1 pint rich soup stock
1 tablespoon lemon juice
¼ bay leaf
¼ teaspoon thyme
Pepper
Salt

1. Sauté the onion and sweet pepper in the butter for 5 minutes, stirring.
2. When the butter is brown, add the flour and stir until brown and smooth.
3. Gradually add the soup stock, stirring constantly. Cook until smooth and thick. Add the lemon juice and seasonings.

Variations
Mushroom Sauce: Add 3 or 4 mushrooms, chopped and cooked in butter.

Sauce Piquant: Add ¼ cup (60 ml) coarsely chopped olives or piccalilli.

Game Sauce: Add ½ cup (125 ml) melted currant jelly.

Sausage

Sausage Meat

Yields 20 pounds (9 kg)

5 pounds (2¼ kg) fat pork meat
15 pounds (6¾ kg) lean pork
½ cup (125 ml) salt
½ tablespoon red pepper
1½ tablespoons black pepper
2½ tablespoons ground sage

1. Run the meat twice through a meat grinder.
2. Add the seasonings, and mix thoroughly.
3. Place in a storage container and refrigerate until needed.

Sausage Loaf

Serves 4–6

1½ pounds (¾ kg) sausage meat
½ cup (125 ml) milk
1½ cups (375 ml) bread or cracker crumbs
1 tablespoon onion, finely chopped
2 tablespoons tomato catsup
2 tablespoons horseradish
½ teaspoon dry mustard
1 egg

1. Heat the oven to 350°F/175°C.
2. Mix all the ingredients and mold as a loaf.
3. Place on a rack in a baking pan and bake uncovered for 1 hour. Serve with a tomato sauce.

Baked Squash with Sausage

Serves 4

2 winter squashes (acorn or small buttercup)
Sausage meat

1. Heat the oven to 350°F/175°C.
2. Cut each squash in halves, remove the seeds, and place facedown in a greased baking dish. Bake for 15 minutes.
3. Turn up the oven temperature to 375°F/190°C.
4. Turn the squash faceup and fill the cavities with the sausage meat. Place in the oven and cook until the sausage is well done, about 45 minutes.

Baked Stuffed Apples

Serves 4

4 apples
Pork sausage meat

1. Heat the oven to 325°F/160°C
2. Pare and core the apples. Fill the cavities with the pork sausage.
3. Cover and bake for 1 hour or until the apples are tender and the sausage is thoroughly cooked.

Lamb

Roast Leg of Lamb

Serves 4–6

4- to 5-pound (2- to 2¼-kg) leg of lamb
Salt and pepper
Flour

1. Heat the oven to 450°F/230°C.
2. Sprinkle the lamb with the salt and pepper, and rub well with the flour. Place on a rack in an open baking pan, skin side down.
3. Roast uncovered for 30 minutes. Reduce the temperature to 300°F/150°C and cook for another 2–2½ hours. If the fat covering is thin, lay several strips of bacon on top and reduce the heat after 20 minutes.

Lamb Croquettes

Serves 4–6

4 cups (1000 ml) chopped cooked lamb roast
½ cup (125 ml) milk
1 cup (250 ml) raisins
1 teaspoon salt
2 eggs, beaten
1 cup (250 ml) cracker crumbs
Cream sauce with peas

1. Mix the lamb, milk, raisins, and salt thoroughly, and shape into croquettes. Roll in the egg and then in the crumbs.
2. Deep-fat fry in oil at 375°–385°F/190°–195°C until a golden brown. Drain on brown paper.
3. Serve with a cream sauce to which peas have been added.

Lamb Curry

Serves 4–6

1½–2 pounds (¾–1 kg) lean lamb or mutton
Flour
Salt and pepper
1 cup (250 ml) water
1 cup (250 ml) shredded onion
1 cup (250 ml) diced celery stalks and leaves
1 tablespoon chopped parsley
2 tablespoons butter
2–3 tablespoons flour
⅛ teaspoon curry powder
3 cups (750 ml) boiled rice

1. Cut the meat in 1-inch (2½-cm) cubes. Dredge with the flour seasoned with the salt and pepper.
2. In a frying pan with a small amount of oil, lightly brown the cubes. Add 1 cup (250 ml) water and simmer. During the cooking, add the onion, celery, and parsley, and additional salt and pepper to taste. Simmer about 30 minutes or until the meat is tender.
3. Strain off the liquor and thicken with the butter, flour, curry powder, and salt. Return the gravy to the pan with the meat, reheat, and serve with a border of rice.

Special Organs

Liver with Sour Cream Gravy

Serves 4–6

6 slices bacon
6 slices calf's liver
Flour
Salt and pepper
1 cup (250 ml) sour cream

1. Fry the bacon in a frying pan until crisp and remove to a hot platter.
2. Trim the liver and dredge with the flour seasoned with the salt and pepper. Fry the liver in the bacon fat slowly at low heat for 15 minutes, turning as necessary. Cover and steam for 5 minutes. Place on a platter with the bacon.
3. Add the sour cream to the drippings and cook for 5–10 minutes, stirring until blended. Season the gravy and pour around the meat.

Liver Patties or Liver Loaf

Serves 4–6

1 pound (½ kg) liver
¼ pound (100 g) bacon
Salt and pepper
Sage
3 crackers, crumbled
1 small onion, chopped
½ cup (125 ml) thick tomato pulp
1 egg (optional)

1. Put the liver and bacon through a food grinder. Season with the salt, pepper, and sage to taste.
2. Add the crackers, onion, and tomato pulp. Mix all thoroughly and form into flat cakes.
3. Fry lightly in hot oil, or bake as a loaf, adding 1 egg to help bind the mixture, for 1½ hours in the oven at 325°F/160°C.

Baked Stuffed Heart

Serves 4–6

1 beef, veal, or pork heart
Bread dressing
Salt and pepper
Flour

1. Heat the oven to 350°F/175°C.
2. Wash the heart and remove the valves and arteries. Stuff with the bread dressing. Rub with the salt and pepper, roll in the flour, and brown in hot drippings or fat. Place in a roasting pan and pour in a little boiling water. Cover tightly.
3. Bake for about 2 hours of slow cooking for beef heart, 1½ hours for calf or pork hearts. If baked in an uncovered pan, baste every 15 minutes. When the heart is tender, remove it from the roasting pan and thicken the remaining liquid to serve as gravy.

Baked Tongue

Serves 4–6

4–4½ pounds (2–3 kg) fresh beef tongue
Beef stock or water
Salt
4–6 peppercorns
6 ounces (180 ml) currant jelly
½ cup (125 ml) chili sauce

1. In a covered saucepan, simmer the tongue in water or beef stock for 3–4 hours or until tender. Salt to taste and add the peppercorns. Let the tongue cool in the stock (just enough to handle comfortably), and then skin. Reserve the stock.
2. Heat the oven to 350°F/175°C.
3. Place the tongue in a small roaster or covered baking dish. Add a small quantity of the stock in which the tongue has been boiled (1–1½ cups/250–375 ml), the jelly, and chili sauce. Bake for 35–45 minutes, basting often, and serve.

Brain Oysters

Serves 4–6

1 calf's brain
Salt
1 tablespoon vinegar
2 eggs, beaten
1 tablespoon milk
Bread crumbs
Hard-cooked egg (optional)
Parsley (optional)

1. Let the brain stand in cold water about 1 hour. Drain and cook for 20 minutes in boiling water to which the salt and vinegar have been added. Drain and cool.
2. Separate the brain into pieces about the size of a large oyster. Blend the eggs and milk in a bowl. Dip the "oysters" in the egg mixture, then roll in the bread crumbs; dip again in the egg and again in the crumbs.
3. Deep-fat fry in oil at 385°–390°F/195°–200°C until golden brown. Serve hot. A garnish of chopped hard-cooked egg and parsley may be added.

Breaded Kidney

Serves 4

4 kidneys
2 teaspoons salt
1 egg, beaten
Bread crumbs

1. Remove the tissue and fat from the kidneys. Cover with water and simmer uncovered for 20 minutes. Remove from the heat, drain, and dry.
2. Season the kidneys with ¼ teaspoon salt to each kidney. Drop them in the beaten egg and roll in the bread crumbs.
3. Sauté until brown in a frying pan with just a little oil, and serve.

Chicken

Roasting Chicken

1. Prepare a whole chicken for roasting by rinsing thoroughly, and rubbing the inside with salt. Fill with stuffing, both the neck and lower opening.
2. Truss or tie in a shape so that the outside presents a compact surface. Cut off the neck bones but leave the skin, which is folded onto the back. Close the neck opening by sewing or lacing string across skewers or toothpicks that are stuck in each side. Fold the wings across the back, over the neck skin. The lower opening will be covered if the drumsticks are crossed and tied down to the tail or slipped into the band of skin below the tail.
3. Rub the skin with butter, and sprinkle with salt and pepper. Place breast-side down on a rack in an open roasting pan. Brown in a hot oven at 450°F/230°C. Reduce the heat to 375°F/190°C and continue roasting uncovered until done, basting frequently. The bird is done if on piercing a thigh near the breast there is no reddish tinge to the juices, or when joints are loose enough to move easily. Remove the string or skewers before serving.

68

Dressing

Yields 1 pound (½ kg)

½ cup (125 ml) butter
1 cup (250 ml) hot water
1-pound (½-kg) loaf stale bread, cubed
1 tablespoon sage
1 tablespoon salt
1 teaspoon pepper
1 cup (250 ml) chopped celery tops and upper
    stalks
2 tablespoons chopped onion

Mix the butter with the hot water and pour over the bread. Add the seasonings, celery, and onion, and mix. This is a dry, flaky dressing that holds together, but the cubed bread does not entirely lose its shape.

Variations

Bacon Dressing: Use ⅓ cup (80 ml) chopped bacon in place of the butter.
Giblet Dresssing: Boil the giblets, chop, and add to the rest of the dressing.
Oyster Dressing: Add 1 pint (500 ml) oysters and omit the celery.
Sausage And Chestnut Dressing: Add ¼ pound (100 g) sausage meat and 2 dozen boiled, shelled, and chopped chestnuts. Decrease the butter to ¼ cup (60 ml).

Boiled Chicken

Serves 4–6

1 chicken
1 bay leaf
2 slices of onion
1 tablespoon salt
2–3 quarts (2–3 l) boiling water

1. Cut the chicken in pieces for serving. Put the chicken pieces in a kettle with the bay leaf, onion slices, and salt, and add the boiling water, enough to cover.
2. Cover the kettle and simmer slowly for 2–2½ hours or until the meat pulls away easily from the bones. Reserve the broth.

Note: A young chicken may be done in 1–1½ hours. Older fowl require longer cooking times, up to 3–4 hours.

Chicken Pie

Serves 4–6

1 boiled chicken and broth
Flour
Milk
Salt and pepper
Biscuit dough (see recipe on page 30)

1. Heat the oven to 425°F/220°C.
2. Prepare the Boiled Chicken as directed above. Remove the flesh from the bones. Thicken the broth with the flour, milk, and seasonings. Add the chicken cut in neat pieces to the thickened broth and put in a baking dish. Be generous with the amount of broth.
3. Roll the biscuit dough about ½ inch (1 cm) thick and cut a piece to fit the top of the baking dish. Cut a round from the center to let out the steam.
4. Place the biscuit dough on top and bake uncovered until the biscuits are golden brown. Bake the rest of the dough as biscuits for second servings.

Creamed Chicken

Serves 4–6

3 tablespoons chicken fat or butter
3 tablespoons cornstarch or ⅓ cup (80 ml) flour
1½ cups (375 ml) chicken broth
1½ cups (375 ml) condensed milk or cream
2 cups (500 ml) boiled chicken, cut in strips
½ cup (125 ml) pimentos, cut in strips
2 egg yolks, beaten
2 teaspoons paprika
Salt and pepper
Toast

1. In a large saucepan, melt the fat. Add the cornstarch and blend.
2. Mix together the chicken broth and condensed milk, and add, stirring until thick.
3. Add the chicken, pimentos, egg yolks, paprika, and salt and pepper to taste. Heat thoroughly and serve on toast.

Chicken Mousse

Serves 6–8

1 tablespoon gelatin
¼ cup (60 ml) cold water
½ cup (125 ml) hot chicken stock
2 cups (500 ml) chicken, chopped
1 tablespoon pickle relish
½ cup (125 ml) chopped celery
¼ teaspoon pepper
1 teaspoon salt
⅛ teaspoon paprika
1 cup (250 ml) heavy cream
Chopped hard-boiled eggs
Pimentos

1. Soak the gelatin in the cold water, and then dissolve in the hot chicken stock. Cool.
2. Combine the chicken with the pickle relish, celery, and seasonings, and add to the gelatin.
3. Whip the cream, fold into the other ingredients. Put into a mold and let harden (chill until firm).
4. Unmold and garnish with the chopped hard-boiled eggs and pimentos cut in ribbons.

Chicken Loaf

Serves 8

1⅓ (325 ml) cups milk, scalded
5 tablespoons butter
2 cups (500 ml) soft bread crumbs or mashed
  potatoes
2 cups (500 ml) cooked chopped chicken
2 eggs, beaten
1 tablespoon chopped parsley or pimento
2 tablespoons chopped green pepper
1 teaspoon onion juice

1. Heat the oven to 350°F/175°C.
2. Mix all the ingredients and pour into a greased loaf pan.
3. Bake for 30–35 minutes with the pan set in a water bath. Unmold and serve with mushrooms, peas, or tomato sauce.

Fish

Cooking Fish

Use a moderate temperature.
To fry, roll in cornmeal or flour, brown first in a small amount of fat in a hot skillet, then finish cooking slowly in an uncovered skillet.
When baking, use a moderate oven.
When cooked in water, simmer rather than boil.
If the fish is fat, it may be baked or broiled satisfactorily. If quite lean, use strips of bacon or other fat on top during baking, or it may be baked with milk or cream.

Baked Whitefish

Serves 4–6

1 whitefish, or large fillet
1 teaspoon salt
1¼ cups sour cream
2 tablespoons bread crumbs
Sliced tomatoes (optional)

1. Heat the oven to 450°F/230°C.
2. Clean the fish and rub it with the salt. Lay on a well-greased baking dish. Bake for 5 minutes, then reduce the temperature to 350°F/175°C.
3. Cover the fish with the sour cream and sprinkle with the bread crumbs. Bake until the sour cream becomes a rich yellow color and the crumbs are brown.
4. Surround the fish on the serving platter with sliced tomatoes or serve with scalloped tomatoes.

Salmon Soufflé

Serves 4–6

2 tablespoons butter
3 tablespoons flour
¼ teaspoon pepper
¼ teaspoon salt
1½ cups (375 ml) milk
1 tablespoon minced parsley
1 teaspoon grated onion
2 cups (500 ml) flaked salmon
3 eggs, yolks and whites separated

1. Heat the oven to 375°F/190°C.
2. Make a white sauce using the butter, flour, pepper, salt, and milk. Add the minced parsley, onion, and fish.

3. Beat the egg yolks lightly and add. Beat the egg whites and fold in.
4. Bake in buttered baking dish about 30 minutes, or until firm in the center.

Salmon Loaf

Serves 4–6

1 can salmon, 14¾ ounces (418 grams)
½ cup (125 ml) milk
½–1 cup (125–250 ml) soft bread crumbs
2 eggs, beaten
2 tablespoons melted butter
Juice of ½ lemon
Salt and pepper

1. Heat the oven to 450°F/230°C.
2. Remove the skin and bones from the salmon and flake.
3. Heat the milk and stir in the bread crumbs to make a paste. Add this to the salmon with the egg, butter, lemon juice, and seasonings.
4. Put in a well-greased baking dish and bake for 35 minutes. Serve hot with egg sauce or parsley sauce.

Tuna Fish Pudding

Serves 4–6

1½ cups (375 ml) milk
½ cup (125 ml) bread crumbs
3 tablespoons butter, melted
1 teaspoon chopped parsley
1 teaspoon chopped onions
⅛ teaspoon salt
¾ cup (185 ml) canned tuna fish
2 eggs

1. Heat the oven to 350°F/175°C.
2. Mix the milk, bread crumbs, butter, parsley, onions, and salt in a saucepan and bring to scald. Add the finely flaked tuna. Break the eggs into the mixture and beat thoroughly.
3. Pour into a casserole and bake for 30–35 minutes.

74

Pike With Horseradish Sauce

Serves 4–6

Fish
2-pound (1-kg) pike
¼ teaspoon white vinegar
1 tablespoon salt

Horseradish Sauce
2 cups (500 ml) fish broth
2 tablespoons butter
2 teaspoons grated horseradish
2 tablespoons flour
1–2 tablespoons water
½ cup (125 ml) cream

Garnish
Lemon slices
Parsley sprigs

1. After the dressed pike has been thoroughly washed, bend the tail toward the mouth and fix it there with a toothpick so that the fish forms a circle. Place it, complete with scales and head, back downward, in a pot. Pour over the pike a sufficient amount of water to cover. Add the vinegar and salt. Cook slowly for 20–30 minutes.
2. To prepare the sauce, pour the fish broth into a skillet. Add the butter and horseradish. Mix the flour with a little water and stir it into the sauce while cooking. More flour may be added to thicken, if necessary. Pour in the cream.
3. Lift the pike carefully from the pot and remove the scales and skin delicately, allowing the head to remain intact. Place on a platter back up, pour the sauce over the fish, and garnish with the slices of lemon and sprigs of parsley. Serve hot.

Salted and Smoked Fish

Codfish and mackerel are two popular salted fish, good standbys in a farm home. If salted and dried, as codfish, freshen by soaking several hours, or overnight in cold water, changing the water two or three times. If put in a brine, as mackerel, freshen by soaking to remove the excess salt. Keep what fish is left covered by the brine to prevent spoilage.

Creamed Mackerel

Serves 2

2 cups (500 ml) cooked mackerel
2 cups (500 ml) medium white sauce
2 hard-cooked eggs, sliced
Parsley

1. Freshen the mackerel as directed above and simmer in fresh water for 20 minutes or until tender. Drain and flake the fish.
2. Add the hard-cooked eggs and the fish to the white sauce (see recipe on page 60). Mix gently.
3. Let all stand in a warm place until the flavors are blended. Sprinkle with the chopped parsley, and serve.

Codfish Cakes

Serves 4–6

1 cup (250 ml) flaked codfish
3 cups (750 ml) raw potatoes, diced
¼ cup (60 ml) milk
1 egg, beaten
1 tablespoon butter
Pepper
Eggs, beaten
Bread crumbs

1. Combine the freshened but uncooked codfish with the potatoes and simmer, not boil, for 20–25 minutes or until the potatoes are tender.
2. Drain and mash, adding the milk, egg, butter, and pepper to taste. Add salt, if more is needed. Let stand until cold.
3. Shape into cakes, dip in the egg and bread crumbs. Brown in drippings in the frying pan.

Note: If the codfish is cooked beforehand, this dish may be made by mixing the flaked cooked fish with leftover mashed potatoes. If the mixture seems dry, add more milk.

Braised Fillet of Finnan Haddie

Serves 4–6

2 pounds (1 kg) finnan haddie fillets (smoked
  haddock)
2 cups (500 ml) diced onions
2 cups (500 ml) diced celery
Pepper and salt
Paprika

1. Cover the fillets with boiling water and let stand
for 10 minutes.
2. Heat the oven to 325°F/160°C.
3. Pour off the water and place one fillet at the
bottom of a casserole or small roaster. Cover it with
the onions, celery, and seasoning to taste. Place over
it the other fillet; season and cover.
4. Bake for 25–30 minutes or until the fish and vegetables are tender. The two fillets may be skewered
together with toothpicks.

Secrets *of* Deep-fat Frying

by Mabel K. Ray

The key to making wholesome fried foods is to have the fat at the correct temperature. That is, the fat must be hot enough when the food is put into it to form a crust on the food immediately so that grease will not be absorbed. Heat the fat gradually.

foods, but are themselves being broken down into substances which are irritating to the digestive organs. This is a permanent "break down" of the fat which can never be reclaimed; it is no longer the original fat but an entirely different chemical substance.

Right Temperature for Frying

The sure way to get the right temperature is to use a thermometer. The second best method of testing temperature of fat is the bread cube test. A 1-inch cube of bread from a slice is dropped into the deep fat. If it turns brown in 40 seconds (which indicates 360–400°F/180–205°C), the temperature of the fat is right to fry cooked foods such as meat or vegetable croquettes, since they really need only to be browned.

For uncooked foods, the fat should be a trifle less hot in order to give the food time to cook through. When a cube of bread turns brown in 60 seconds (335–360°F/170–180°C), the temperature is right for such foods.

"But," you may say, "I was taught that when the fat started smoking it was hot enough to use for frying." That is a serious mistake! For when fats smoke, they are not only hot enough to burn

To Prevent Fat Absorption

One trick used to prevent fat absorption is that of covering croquettes or slices of fruit with a substance which will form a coating quickly when it comes in contact with hot fat. Dipping in egg and crumbs and the use of a cover batter are two methods.

Foods such as doughnuts, which have egg and flour in them, need no additional treatment. Of course, cooked mixtures must be held in shape with a binding material such as a thick white sauce or a tapioca mixture. The food should be as dry as possible on the outside and not too juicy inside, since moist surfaces lengthen the time it takes to form a crust. It is well to remember, also, that rich batters and doughs absorb more fat than others.

To Keep the Fat at the Right Temperature

In order not to lower the temperature

of the fat too much a small number of pieces should be fried at one time. This is especially true when French-frying potatoes, since they are naturally wet and cold. With the wire frying basket one uses to lower the food slowly into the hot fat, this problem is easily met. Having the food at room temperature before frying also helps.

Cooking Time

The length of time the food should be cooked is determined largely by color. When the food is golden brown all over, remove it and drain on absorbent paper.

Fats for Deep Frying

"What kind of fat is best to use for deep frying?" That's a long story since there are so many excellent cooking oils and fats, including cottonseed, corn and other vegetable oils; nut oils; lard and other animal fats. To be good for deep frying, a fat should allow the food fried to keep its flavor and tint give it its fatty taste. The fat should take up no flavors, it should heat to a high temperature without smoking or scorching, and it should be usable again.

Of the animal fats, lard is the best to use for deep-fat frying. However, it smokes more quickly than the vegetable fats. The smoking temperature varies a good deal with the size of the vessel, the surface exposed, and the amount of foreign matter present. A deep iron or heavy aluminum kettle is best to use.

Vegetables

Vegetables offer one of the best ways to make meals attractive. They add color, contrast in texture and flavor, and much in food value. Without the regular use of a wide variety of vegetables, meals lack both interest and proper protection.

Minerals, vitamins, and roughage are furnished by vegetables, the amount varying with kind. Here are a few general rules which may help in selecting and preparing vegetables:

* Colorful vegetables are the best sources of vitamins and in most cases of minerals.

* Minerals and vitamins seem to lie close to the skin, so unnecessary paring is wasteful in more than one way.

* Minerals and vitamins are lost through cooking overlong, or if water for cooking is used to excess, or if the vegetable is cut in very small pieces.

Serve raw vegetables frequently in salads or as relishes.

—*The Farmer's Wife*

Asparagus and Eggs

2 cups (500 ml) medium white sauce
⅛ teaspoon pepper
2 cups (500 ml) asparagus, canned or freshly
  cooked
4 hard-cooked eggs
Buttered crumbs

1. Heat the oven to 350°F/175°C.
2. Make the white sauce (see recipe on page 60) with the pepper.
3. Alternate layers of the asparagus and white sauce in a greased baking dish.
4. Cut the eggs in halves, lengthwise, and put over the top. Top with the buttered crumbs.
5. Bake for 20 minutes or until thoroughly heated.

Baked Celery and Carrots

1. Heat the oven to 350°F/175°C.
2. Cut some outside stalks of celery into small pieces. Peel some carrots and slice. Combine the vegetables in a baking dish with beef stock, evaporated milk, or cream to half-fill the dish, and season.
3. Cover and bake for 25 minutes or until the carrots are tender.

Corn Fritters with Bacon

Bacon and bacon fat
¼ cup (60 ml) flour
½ teaspoon baking powder
½ teaspoon salt
2 cups (500 ml) canned or cooked corn
2 eggs, slightly beaten
1½ teaspoons melted butter
Maple syrup (optional)

1. Fry some bacon and keep it warm while making the corn fritters. Reserve the bacon fat.
2. Sift the dry ingredients. Mix with the corn, eggs, and butter into a thick batter. Drop by spoonfuls on a hot griddle, greased with the bacon fat. Let brown on one side and get light before turning.
3. Serve with crisp slices of bacon on top and maple syrup if desired.

Baked Lima Beans

1 cup (250 ml) dry lima beans
¾ cup (185 ml) bacon, diced
½ cup (125 ml) chopped onion
1 cup (250 ml) strained tomatoes
¼ teaspoon pepper
½ teaspoon salt
½ teaspoon paprika
2 tablespoons flour

1. Cover the beans with water and soak overnight.
2. Drain the beans and cover with fresh water. Heat to boiling, boil for 5 minutes, and remove from the heat. Let stand for 1 hour. Add water, if necessary, and simmer uncovered for approximately 45 minutes or until nearly tender.
3. Heat the oven to 350°F/175°C.
4. Brown the bacon in a frying pan and add the onions. Add the tomatoes, seasonings, and flour. Cook together for a few minutes before adding the beans.
5. Bake uncovered for 50 minutes or until tender.

Boston Baked Beans

4 cups (1000 ml) navy beans
1 small onion
¼ pound (100 g) salt pork
½–1 tablespoon salt
½ tablespoon mustard
3 tablespoons molasses
1 cup (250 ml) hot water

1. Wash and soak the beans in cold water overnight.
2. In the morning drain, cover with fresh water, and simmer uncovered for 45–50 minutes or until the skins break. Drain.
3. Heat the oven to 250°F/120°C.
4. Place the onion in the bottom of earthenware bean pot, pour in the beans.
5. Score the rind of the salt pork. Mix the seasonings, molasses, and hot water together. Bury the pork in the beans, leaving the rind exposed. Add the molasses and hot water mixture.
6. Cover the bean pot and bake for 6–8 hours. Add water from time to time when necessary. Bake uncovered for the last hour.

Harvard Beets

2 cups (500 ml) beets, canned or fresh
⅓ cup (80 ml) sugar
1 tablespoon cornstarch
½ cup (125 ml) vinegar and beet juice
½ teaspoon salt
2 tablespoons butter

1. Slice or dice the beets into small pieces.
2. To make a sauce, mix the sugar and cornstarch, add the rest of the ingredients, and boil, stirring until thick and smooth.
3. Add the beets and let stand on the back of the range for several minutes.

Baked Sweet Potatoes and Apples

4 cups (1000 ml) pared and sliced sweet potatoes
4 cups (1000 ml) sliced apples
1 teaspoon salt
2 slices lemon
2 slices orange
2 cloves
2 cups (500 ml) brown sugar

1. Heat the oven to 400°F/205°C.
2. Place all the ingredients without extra water in a covered baking dish. Bake for 1 hour or until the potatoes are tender.
3. Remove the orange and cloves. If the apples are very juicy, drain off the juice, boil it down, and pour it over the casserole before serving. Delicious with roast pork.

Potato Puff

4 cups (1000 ml) hot mashed potatoes
1 tablespoon melted butter
2 tablespoons milk
1 tablespoon salt
¼ teaspoon pepper
Yolks of 2 eggs
Whites of 2 eggs, beaten stiff

1. Heat the oven to 375°F/190°C.
2. Mix all the ingredients but the whites of the eggs in the order given and beat thoroughly. Fold in the stiffly beaten whites.
3. Pile in a buttered baking dish and bake for 20–25 minutes or until the mixture puffs and is brown on

the top. This mixture is excellent as a border for planked steak or browned meat on a heatproof platter.

Sweet Potato Croquettes

6 medium-size sweet potatoes
⅓ cup (80 ml) evaporated milk, scalded
4 tablespoons butter
2 tablespoons brown sugar
Salt to taste
1 egg, beaten slightly
1 cup (250 ml) bread crumbs, sifted
Melted butter

1. Boil the potatoes until tender. Peel and mash.
2. Heat the oven to 350°F/175°C.
3. To the mashed sweet potatoes, add the milk, butter, sugar, and salt to taste. Whip until thoroughly mixed and somewhat fluffy.
4. Form into cone-shaped croquettes. Dip in the egg and sifted toasted crumbs. Place in a sheet cake pan or on a baking sheet and brush with the butter. Bake uncovered for 30 minutes.

Note: To vary, insert a marshmallow in the center of each croquette.

Scalloped Tomatoes

4 cups (1000 ml) sliced tomatoes
1 teaspoon salt
1 cup (250 ml) thick cream, sweet or sour
2 cups (500 ml) bread cubes, toasted

1. Heat the oven to 350°F/175°C.
2. Put a layer of the tomatoes in a buttered baking dish. Season with a pinch of the salt, add part of the cream, then a layer of the bread cubes. Repeat the layers, until all the ingredients are used up.
3. Bake for 25–30 minutes or until hot through and brown on top.

Variations

Without Cream: Omit the cream and use bits of butter on each layer of crumbs.
With Onions: Parboil three or four sliced onions for 15 minutes. Drain. Alternate in layers with the tomatoes and bread cubes. Bake until the onions are tender.

Baked Stuffed Tomatoes or Green Peppers

6 ripe tomatoes or 6 green peppers
1 cup (250 ml) minced ham, chicken, or beef
½ cup (125 ml) diced celery
1 teaspoon chopped onion
½ cup (125 ml) bread crumbs
½ cup (125 ml) tomato pulp or thick cream
1 teaspoon salt

1. Heat the oven to 350°F/175°C.
2. Scoop out the insides of the tomatoes or peppers. Reserve the tomato pulp. Parboil the peppers in boiling, salted water for 10 minutes
3. Combine the other ingredients. Fill the peppers or tomato shells with the mixture.
4. Bake uncovered for approximately 45 minutes.

Variation

Vegetable Filling: Substitute corn for the meat. Use part of the scooped-out tomato pulp in place of half the celery.

Scalloped and Au Gratin Vegetables

Many vegetables may be scalloped with white, cheese, or tomato sauce.
2–2½ cups (500–624 ml) cooked or canned vegetable
1 cup (250 ml) sauce
Bread crumbs, buttered

1. Heat the oven to 350°F/175°C.
2. Drain the vegetable and reserve the vegetable liquor, if desired. (The vegetable liquor may be used in place of part of the milk or tomato in the sauce.)
3. Make the sauce. See recipes for "Sauces for Meats and Vegetables" on pages 60–61.
2. Alternate the vegetable and sauce in a buttered baking dish and top with buttered crumbs.
3. Bake until the crumbs are brown.

Variations

(Two or three vegetables may be combined in one dish.)
With Cheese Sauce: Potatoes, cabbage, cauliflower, parsnips, onions, turnips, asparagus, spinach.
With Cream or Rich White Sauce: Any of the above, also carrots, salsify, or oyster plant.
With Tomato Sauce: Dried or green beans, celery, onions.

Savory Sauerkraut

1. Heat the sauerkraut with butter, pork or bacon fat, or thick cream, sweet or sour (¼ cup/60 ml melted fat or ½ cup/125 ml cream to 1 quart/1 l kraut).
2. Simmer until the excess moisture is removed and serve. Additional seasonings may be used, such as paprika, celery seed, caraway seed.

Vegetable Ring or Custard

2 tablespoons butter
1½ cups (375 ml) milk, scalded
3 eggs, slightly beaten
1½ cups (375 ml) raw or cooked vegetable
1 teaspoon salt

1. Heat the oven to 350°F/175°C.
2. In a saucepan, heat the butter with the milk. Add the other ingredients.
3. Pour into individual custard cups or a ring mold. Set in a larger pan of hot water. Bake like a custard for 45 minutes to 1 hour. Unmold.

Variations
Raw Vegetables: Carrot, or finely shredded or ground turnip, or spinach run through a food chopper. With the ground spinach use only 1 cup (250 ml) milk.

Cooked Vegetables: Carrot, turnip, spinach, asparagus, corn, or celery, cooked and finely chopped.
Spinach With Cheese Sauce: Bake the above custard mixture in individual custards, using spinach as the vegetable. Unmold and serve with a cheese sauce (see recipe on page 60).

Use Butter Generously

by Miriam Williams

Some women are naturally lavish. They set a good table— plenty of maple syrup and butter for the "stack o' wheats," an extra dish of sauce beside dessert, a full jar of crisp butter cookies.

Other women use creamery butter sparingly, usually buying a reliable brand of butter substitute, because it is "just as good."

The butter-saving woman is not as scientific or wise a planner as it might seem if she looks to a cream check for cash. Multiply butter-saving and butter-substituting country cooks many times and it does something to the national supply of butter. I learned that the holdings of butter in cold storage were higher last August than during 1929, which marked the record peak of 151 million pounds. Folks must use butter a bit more freely if a surplus such as this is to be reduced and the price of butter kept stable.

Fats which are competitive to butter all have their place, but one does not yearn to be particularly lavish with them.

With butter it is different. I level-measure baking powder, spice, flour for cakes or gravy, but when it comes to measuring butter for seasoning, it's a rounding table-spoonful or a generous lump. Few things make me bristle like the restaurant sandwich which isn't spread with butter, and clear to the edges, too.

The dairyman who almost caused a rift in the church by his explosions over the "measurably skimpy" pats of butter which the ladies' aid served at the church supper, has my sympathy.

Let yourself go when it comes to seasoning with butter. Folks always sit up with relish to the family table where there are melting butter squares on hot porterhouse or round steak and a golden yellow heart in the bowl of fluffy mashed potatoes. And who can resist vegetables cooked just to a tenderness, their own liquid cooked down, and seasoned with sweet flavored butter? Rich velvety cakes made with butter command a premium at the market or church bazaar.

Use generously of your own products. Set a good table, cook well so that you may live well. *The Farmer's Wife* magazine recipes support these ideas.

Chapter 6

Hot Supper Dishes

Here's where you'll find the recipe for that dish without meat or that combination dish which seems to suit the lighter meal, whether it's supper, lunch, or a light dinner. Many of these dishes are ideal for carrying to a get-together dinner, or to leave at home for the men who must get their own. Many of the supper dishes are really a meal-in-one. They are often adapted to platter or casserole style of serving which simplifies dishes and serving.

If you are troubled about what to do with leftovers, what to serve to save time and dishes, how to combine those foods which do not seem to belong to any one group, study this section carefully. Egg and cheese dishes are included here, although they are often used in other meals as well. Additional dishes suited for supper are found in other sections, such as main dish salads and many of the hearty vegetable dishes.

—*The Farmer's Wife*

Egg Supper Dishes

Cook eggs at a low temperature for best results. Simmering or below boiling temperature for soft- and hard-cooked eggs; fairly slow cooking for scrambled and poached eggs, and omelets; slow to moderate oven for sponge and angel cakes, meringues, and custard.

Soft-Cooked Eggs

* Method 1: Place the eggs in a saucepan with enough water to cover. Bring to the boiling point slowly. Remove the eggs and serve.
* Method 2: Coddled eggs: Place the eggs in a saucepan and cover with boiling water. Cover the pan and let stand on back of the stove for 8–10 minutes.

Hard-Cooked Eggs

* Method 1: Place the eggs as for coddled eggs. Let stand where the water will keep hot but will not boil, for 40–45 minutes.
* Method 2: Cover the eggs in a saucepan with boiling water; let simmer gently for 8 minutes.

Poached Eggs

1. Use a shallow pan with enough water to cover the eggs. Let the water boil. Remove the pan to the back of the stove.
2. Break each egg separately into a saucer and slip gently into the water.
3. Remove when the white is firm and a film covers the yolk. A skimmer or pancake turner may be used to remove the eggs. Drain and serve on toast.

Note: Vinegar or lemon juice in the water help keep the white from spreading. Eggs may also be poached in milk or bouillon.

Scrambled Eggs

5 eggs
½ cup (125 ml) milk
½ teaspoon salt
⅛ teaspoon pepper
2 tablespoons butter or bacon fat
Garnishes: Parsley, jelly, a bit of butter and paprika, bacon strips, asparagus, tomato sauce, Spanish sauce.

1. Beat the eggs slightly. Add the milk, salt, and pepper.
2. Melt the butter in an omelet pan or heavy skillet. Turn in the egg mixture and cook slowly, scraping from the bottom and sides of the pan as the mixture thickens. Cook until creamy, not dry.
3. Remove from the pan the instant the eggs begin to set. Serve at once.

Puffy Omelet

5 eggs, separated
5 tablespoons water
½ teaspoon salt
Dash of pepper or paprika
2 tablespoons butter

1. Heat the oven to 350°F/175°C.
2. Beat the yolks until thick and lemon colored. Add the water, salt, and pepper or paprika.
3. Beat the egg whites until stiff and fold into the yolk mixture.
4. Melt the butter in a hot omelet pan or skillet over medium heat. Turn in the egg mixture, spread evenly. Reduce the heat and cook slowly, turning the pan and lifting the soft mixture with a spatula so the omelet cooks and browns evenly.
5. When the omlet is well puffed up and a delicate brown underneath, put into the oven to finish cooking the top. When firm to the touch, it is done. Fold with a spatula. Turn out on a hot platter. Serve at once.

Variations

With Vegetables, Cheese or Meat: Before the omelet is folded, place heated vegetables or chopped, cooked meat (as ham or bacon), or grated cheese over one half. Fold and serve.

Spanish Omelet: Add 1 tablespoon finely chopped onion and 1 tablespoon chopped green pepper to the omelet mixture. Cook as directed. Put on a hot platter and pour Spanish sauce over it. (See recipe for Spanish Sauce on page 61.)

When Hens Are Busy

by Gertrude Brown, May 1930

Now that the biddies are through vacationing and the chicks are hatched, 'tis time for the family to have as many eggs to eat as they've been wishing for all winter. Not just fried or hard-cooked eggs until everyone is sick of them, but eggs in all sorts of new dresses and disguises. A hen worth her board and keep produces 20 eggs during the month of May. Thus even a small flock should furnish a generous supply.

Eggs are largely protein which makes them a meat substitute when served straight. In addition, the yolk is very rich in the most usable kind of iron, in vitamin A, otherwise found chiefly in butterfat, and in phosphorus, fat, and vitamins B and D.

The large amount of protein means that eggs must be cooked at low heat if they are not to become leathery and indigestible, which is true whether one is preparing an egg dessert, dressing, sandwich, or salad. When they are cooked in the oven, the temperature should be near the boiling point of water, but never so hot that a pan of water placed alongside would actually boil.

Goldenrod Eggs

1 cup (250 ml) medium white sauce
5 hard-cooked eggs
Toast
Pepper or paprika

1. Make the white sauce (see recipe on page 60).
2. Chop the egg whites and add to the white sauce.
3. Pour the sauce over the toast and top with the egg yolks that have been forced through a ricer. Sprinkle with a dash of pepper or paprika.

Note: This combination may be poured over spinach, chopped meat, or flaked fish for a breakfast or supper dish.

Variations

Creamed Eggs With Bacon: Quarter the whole eggs lengthwise, add to the white sauce, and top with 1 or 2 slices crisp bacon.
Creamed Pimento Eggs: Add ½ cup (125 ml) chopped pimento to creamed whole eggs. Serve on toast.

Hard-Cooked Eggs Au Gratin

2 cups (500 ml) medium white sauce
1 cup (250 ml) soft bread crumbs, divided
6 hard-cooked eggs, quartered
Onion juice to flavor
½ cup (125 ml) grated cheese

1. Heat the oven to 350°F/175°C.
2. Make the white sauce (see recipe on page 60).
3. Butter a baking dish and line with a small amount of the bread crumbs. Pour in a layer of the white sauce, arrange the eggs in the dish, and cover with the remaining white sauce. Add the onion juice if desired. Cover with the grated cheese and the remaining bread crumbs.
4. Bake for 20–25 minutes or until heated through.

Genuine New England Dishes

by Ida S. Harrington, November 1928

"Do send me a dozen or two genuine New England recipes," wrote a friend of mine recently. "I'm so tired of cooking the same old things, and I just can't get away from home right now. Of course, you have them all at hand."

New England recipes all at hand? Little did she realize how they differ from state to state, town to town, family to family. One has only to suggest having found the real original rule for Boston-baked beans or Rhode Island johnny cake to start a buzz of protest from old settlers whose traditional methods differ from those under discussion.

Recipes are family heirlooms. Menus are family rites. If a family has fish cakes for Sunday breakfast all the year except midwinter, when sausages and buckwheat cakes are served, they continue to follow just that schedule year in and year out. If baked beans are served on Saturday night, they are always served on Saturday night. If great-grandmother did not put tomato in her clam chowder, tomato is not included to this day.

But to select a dozen or two New England recipes—obviously there could be no cut-and-dried procedure for obtaining them.

Family tradition would have to be my authority, but the number of families consulted would have to be limited. So I slipped into the kitchens of two old friends and obtained my treasure. From the yellowed leaves of "Aunt Julia's" and "Cousin Sally's" painstaking manuscripts, I chose these recipes. No liberties have been taken with them beyond translating into definite amounts "the blue bowl full" and "right tip to this mark in the chowder kettle," the kettle that has been and will continue to be used "always" and so makes measuring absurd. What a delightful suggestion of permanence!

Clam Chowder

Ingredients
6 slices of salt pork, diced
4 medium-size onions
1 quart (1 l) diced potatoes
1 quart (1 l) clams
1 quart (1 l) milk
4 soda crackers
4 tablespoons butter
Pepper and salt

1. Fry the pork crisp and cut fine as it is being fried. Add the onions and fry, constantly cutting them and being careful not to burn.
2. Put the pork, onions, and pork fat into a chowder kettle, add the diced potatoes, the clam water, and boiling water

to cover. When the potatoes are soft, add the clams from which the black part has been removed and which have been put through the meat chopper (a modern liberty). Cook for 5–10 minutes. Add the seasoning and scalded milk.
3. Into a tureen put the crackers and butter. Pour the hot chowder over them and serve at once, very hot.

Note: A Postmodern Liberty: To prepare the clams for the chowder kettle, put the clams with their own liquor into a graniteware saucepan, bring to a boil, skim out the clams, and reserve the clam liquor (water).

Rhode Island Johnny Cakes
The meal used for these is made from white cap corn, stone ground by water power or wind because this method is slower and does not heat the meal. This is a special Rhode Island meal which is now shipped in small quantities to many localities. It must be used quickly as it soon deteriorates.

1. Put 2 cups (500 ml) of meal into a bowl with 1 teaspoonful of salt. Have the teakettle at the jumping boil and pour boiling water over the meal a little at a time, beating vigorously until the meal is scalded but not thinned. Then thin with milk to the consistency of a drop batter.
2. Drop on a well-greased hot griddle and cook like griddle cakes. For huckleberry Johnny cakes, add ¾ cup (185 ml) of berries to this recipe.

Sallie's Rye Dough Dabs
Ingredients
2 cups (500 ml) rye meal
1 cup (250 ml) flour
3 heaping teaspoons sugar
1 egg

1¼ cups milk
1 teaspoon cream tartar
½ teaspoon soda
Salt

Mix and fry like doughnuts.

Indian Pudding
Ingredients
2 quarts (2 l) milk
1 cup (250 ml) molasses
1 cup (250 ml) Rhode Island meal
1 teaspoon salt
1 teaspoon ginger

1. Put the salt, molasses and ginger in the bottom of a brown earthenware pudding dish.
2. Put 1 quart of the milk in the double boiler and scald. Mix the meal with three-quarters of the cold milk and add to the scalded milk. Boil 1 hour and cool.
3. Then put into the pudding dish with the molasses, etc. Stir well. Bake in a slow oven 2 hours. Then pour over it the reserved cup of cold milk (without stirring) and bake slowly 2 hours more.

Fish Cakes
Ingredients
2 cups (500 ml) salt fish, cooked
6 potatoes
2 tablespoons butter
4 tablespoons milk
1 egg
Pepper

1. Boil potatoes until tender, drain, and mash together with the fish until very light and fine. Add the butter, milk, and egg.
2. Drop by spoonful into hot fat and fry brown.

Cheese Supper Dishes

Cheese Soufflé

¼ cup (60 ml) butter
¼ cup (60 ml) flour
1 cup (250 ml) milk
½ teaspoon salt
⅛ teaspoon cayenne or paprika
¾–1 cup (185–250 ml) grated American cheese
5 eggs, separated

1. Heat the oven to 350°F/175°C.
2. Make a white sauce of the butter, flour, milk, salt, and cayenne.
3. Remove from the heat. Add the cheese and beat until it is melted. Add the beaten egg yolks. Cool slightly.
4. Beat the egg whites until stiff and fold into the cheese mixture.
5. Pour the cheese-egg mixture into a buttered baking dish. Bake in a pan of hot water at 350°F/175°C for about 20 minutes. When done, a knife inserted comes out clean.

Variation
Corn And Cheese Soufflé: Add 1 cup (250 ml) canned or cooked corn and 1 tablespoon butter to the cheese soufflé.

Squash Cheese Soufflé

2 cups (500 ml) mashed winter squash
⅓–½ cup (80–125 ml) cream
2 tablespoons butter
½ cup (125 ml) grated cheese
Salt, pepper
2 eggs, separated

1. Heat the oven to 350°F/175°C.
2. Mix the mashed squash with the cream, butter, cheese, and seasonings. Add the well-beaten egg yolks.
3. Beat the egg whites until stiff but not dry and fold them carefully into the squash mixture.
4. Pour into a greased baking dish, set the dish in a pan of hot water, and bake for 40 minutes.

Rinktum Tiddy

1 pint (500 ml) home-canned tomatoes
¼ teaspoon salt
1 teaspoon pepper
⅛ teaspoon cayenne
1 tablespoon chopped onion
¼ pound (100 g) American cheese
1 teaspoon butter
1 egg, beaten
Toast or crackers

1. Heat the tomatoes, salt, pepper, cayenne, and onion in a skillet. When hot, add the cheese cut in bits, while stirring constantly. When smooth, add the butter and egg.
2. Serve on slices of hot, buttered toast or crackers.

Welsh Rarebit

2 cups (500 ml) medium white sauce
½ pound (250 g) grated cheddar cheese
½ teaspoon paprika
¼ teaspoon mustard
2 eggs or 3–4 yolks, slightly beaten
Toast or crackers

1. Make the white sauce in the top of a double boiler (see recipe on page 60).
2. Set the top of the double boiler over hot, but not boiling, water. Add the cheese and seasonings, stir until smooth. Add the eggs, stirring quickly until blended. Cook and stir 2 or 3 minutes until it thickens a little.
3. Pour over crisp toast or crackers.

Red Bunny

3 tablespoons butter
1 tablespoon finely chopped green pepper or
    pimento
1 tablespoon finely chopped onion
2 tablespoons flour
1 teaspoon salt
¼ teaspoon pepper
¼ teaspoon celery salt
2 cups (500 ml) thick tomato pulp or tomato
    soup
2 eggs, beaten
1 cup (250 ml) finely cut cheese
Toast or crackers

1. Melt the butter in a skillet. Brown the chopped
vegetables in the butter.
2. Add the flour and seasonings, then the tomatoes,
and cook until the mixture thickens slightly.
3. Add the eggs and cook for 1 minute.
4. Add the cheese and stir until melted.
5. Serve hot on toast or crackers.

Cottage Cheese Loaf with Peas

2 cups (500 ml) cottage cheese
1 cup (250 ml) chopped peanuts
1 cup (250 ml) bread crumbs
2 eggs, beaten
¼ teaspoon salt
½ teaspoon baking soda
Bread crumbs
2 tablespoons melted butter
1 cup (250 ml) canned peas, drained

1. Heat the oven to 350°F/175°C.
2. Mix all the ingredients, except the bread crumbs,
butter, and peas.
3. Grease a loaf pan generously and sprinkle with
the bread crumbs. Put in half the mixture, then layer
the peas. Add the balance of the mixture and top
with the melted butter. Bake for 45 minutes.

Cereal Supper Dishes

Spanish Rice with Bacon

6 slices bacon, diced
2 onions, chopped
1 green pepper, chopped
½ teaspoon salt
¼ teaspoon pepper
2 cups (500 ml) tomatoes
2 cups (500 ml) boiled rice

1. Fry the bacon until crisp and remove from the skillet.
2. Add the onions and green pepper to the bacon grease and cook until soft. Add the remaining ingredients and simmer gently until heated through.
3. Turn into a serving dish and sprinkle the bacon on top.

Variations
With Raw Rice: Use 1 cup (250 ml) uncooked rice that has been washed and dried. Brown the rice in the fat with the onions and green pepper, then add the other ingredients as directed and 2 cups (500 ml) water. Cover and cook on top of the stove until the rice is tender.
With Meat: Omit the bacon, but use some fat. Add 1 cup (250 ml) ground beef.

Baked Macaroni with Cheese

2 cups (500 ml) cooked macaroni
1 cup (250 ml) cubed cheddar cheese
1 egg, beaten
Salt and pepper
2 cups (500 ml) milk, scalded

1. Heat the oven to 350°F/175°C.
2. Alternate the macaroni in layers with the cheese in a baking dish.
3. Add the egg and seasonings to the milk and pour in the baking dish almost to the top layer.
4. Bake for 20–25 minutes or until the milk is absorbed and the top is brown.

Variations

With Cheese Sauce: Instead of the milk and egg, make 2 cups (500 ml) medium white sauce (see recipe on page 60). Add the cheese and pour over the macaroni. Top with buttered bread crumbs.

With Celery: Reduce the cheese to ¾ cup (185 ml) and alternate in layers as above, using also 1 cup (250 ml) cooked celery.

Baked Rice And Cheese: Substitute cooked rice for macaroni.

Why Not Hominy?

by Bess M. Rowe, October 1933

Hominy was served often by our pioneer grandmothers, but in some parts of the country at least, we seem to be neglecting it of late. Since it is a common southern dish, we asked our good Extension Department friends in Tennessee how they prepare and use it down there and received this recipe from Miss Oma Worley, a District Home Demonstration Agent. It is a recipe which has been used by her family many times.

Lye Hominy: Southern Style

To make lye: Put into a black iron or enameled vessel 2 gallons (7½ l) of clean wood ashes (hickory preferred), pour over them enough hot water so that when the ashes have been well stirred and allowed to settle there will be about 3 inches (7½ cm) of lye above the ashes.

To make hominy: Select sound corn, shell, and put into an iron or enameled vessel, cover well with boiling water and add 3–4 cups (750–1000 ml) of the lye

(the amount needed varies with strength of the lye, but should be sufficient to turn white corn yellow or yellow corn a deeper yellow as it cooks). Cook 1 hour or more until the skins of the corn will slip; as the corn swells, more hot water may be added. To remove the skins, wash in two or three changes of water, stirring vigorously or rubbing the corn between the hands (at the third washing). The amount of lye then left in gives that real lye hominy flavor that is traditional in the South.

Put the washed corn back into the same vessel, add boiling water and cook until done, requiring 3–4 four hours or 80 minutes at 10 pounds (4½ kg) in a pressure cooker (do not have lye hominy in direct contact with aluminum).

To prepare for serving, season with salt and butter, cook until thoroughly heated—or put into a baking dish, add salt, lay strips of bacon over top and bake. Serve hot.

The best hominy results from cooking it in a black iron pot all night against a banked wood fire in the fireplace. This gives long-time cooking at low heat.

Since it isn't always convenient (or even possible) to make the lye at home, we give you this recipe, using the prepared lye. It is appropriate that it should come from Iowa State College—from the "tall corn" state! The directions are reprinted from an Iowa State College leaflet. If you do not want to make your own hominy, you can purchase it in cans. Whether homemade or ready-canned, it offers welcome variety.

Homemade Hominy

The hominy can be started one day and finished the next. On the first day, carry the process through the different washings, then let stand over night in cold water. The next day, drain off the water, cover with cold water and boil. However, 2 or 3 boilings will be sufficient if the lye has been properly washed off.

Ingredients
2 tablespoons lye
2 cups (500 ml) cold water
1 gallon (3¾ l) boiling water
2 quarts (2 l) shelled corn

1. Put the lye into a kettle and add the cold water. When dissolved, add the boiling water and mix thoroughly.
2. Stir in the corn and bring to the boiling point in 15–20 minutes. Boil for 20 minutes, stirring constantly. If the mixture cooks down so thick that the corn begins to stick to the kettle, add more boiling water. After boiling for 20 minutes, test some corn in cold water. If the eyes (or that part of kernel which has been attached to the ear) fall out when touched, the corn is ready to wash. If the eyes do not come out, boil a few minutes longer and test again.
3. Remove from the stove, fill the kettle with cold water and stir thoroughly. Drain off the water. Repeat 4 or 5 times. A wooden churn dasher is very good to use in the washing, as it loosens the eyes and one does not need to put one's hands in the water. After the lye is washed off, continue working with the corn until the eyes are all out.

4. Cover the corn with cold water and bring to a boil. Drain off. Repeat the same process 3 or 4 times. After the last boiling, cover the corn with cold water, bring to the boiling point, and boil for 3–4 hours. As the corn swells, add more cold water.

Caution: Do not use anything but an iron kettle and stir with a paddle. When washing the hominy, do not put the hands into the first 4 wash waters.

Note: If you want to make hominy in quantity, pack the cooked hominy into hot, sterilized cans as you would any product for canning, cover with the liquid in which it was cooked, process for 90 minutes at 10 pounds (4½ kg) pressure or for 3 hours in the water bath.

Hominy Turnover
Ingredients
2 cups (500 ml) cooked hominy
1 cup (250 ml) milk
1 teaspoon salt
2 eggs, well-beaten
1 tablespoon fat

1. Mix all the ingredients, except the fat, together.
2. Turn into a frying pan in which the fat has been melted. Stir until hot throughout. Let it cook until golden brown on the bottom, then fold like an omelet, and serve on a hot platter. This is suitable for the main dish at supper or luncheon.

Baked Hominy And Cheese
2 cups (500 ml) cooked hominy
½ cup (125 ml) grated cheese
Salt and pepper to taste
1 cup (250 ml) milk
1 tablespoon flour
1 tablespoon butter
Bread crumbs

parsley or a small amount of grated cheese may be added.

Scalloped Hominy

Arrange in a baking dish alternate layers of boiled hominy and minced meat or fish or grated cheese. Pour over all 1 cup (250 ml) of white sauce and bake for 30 minutes. This may be used as the principal part of the meat course.

1. In a baking dish, alternate layers of the cooked hominy and cheese. Season with the salt and pepper.
2. Make a white sauce of the milk, flour, and butter. Pour the sauce over the hominy and cheese, cover with the crumbs, dot with the butter, and bake.

Plain Hominy

Cook the hominy, seasoning to taste. Drain and serve in place of potatoes.

Browned Hominy

Cook and drain the hominy. Add butter and brown down slightly. Serve in place of potatoes.

Creamed Hominy

2 tablespoons butter
2 tablespoons flour
2 cups (500 ml) milk
½ teaspoon salt
Pepper
3 cups (750 ml) hominy
Chopped parsley or grated cheese

1. Make a white sauce of the butter, flour, milk, salt, and pepper.
2. Add the hominy and reheat. Chopped

Hominy Loaf

Ingredients
1 cup (250 ml) milk
1 cup (250 ml) soft bread crumbs
1 cup (250 ml) grated cheese
2 eggs, beaten
1 tablespoon green pepper
1 teaspoon onion juice
1 teaspoon salt
1 tablespoon chopped parsley
2 cups (500 ml) hominy

1. Heat the oven to 350°F/175°C.
2. Scald the milk. Add the bread crumbs, cheese, beaten eggs, seasonings, and hominy.
3. Turn into a baking dish, place in a pan of hot water, and bake. Serve with a tomato sauce.

Tomato Sauce: Melt 2 tablespoons butter, add 2 tablespoons flour, ½ teaspoon salt, and ⅛ teaspoon pepper, and blend thoroughly. Cook 1 cup (250 ml) strained tomatoes with a slice of onion and add gradually to the fat and flour. Cook thoroughly. Add ½ tablespoon capers, if desired.

Meat Supper Dishes

Creamed Dried Beef and Peas

¾ cup (185 ml) shredded dried beef
⅓ cup (80 ml) butter or bacon fat
⅓ cup (80 ml) flour
3 cups (750 ml) milk
2 cups (500 ml) cooked peas
Toast
Grated cheese

1. Soak the dried beef in fresh water, if it is very salty, and drain. Shred the beef and frizzle in the fat in a skillet until the edges curl. Remove the beef.
2. Add the flour and milk to the fat to make a gravy.
3. Add the peas and beef and heat through.
4. Serve hot on the toast and sprinkle with the grated cheese.

Variation

Dried Beef Gravy: Prepare as above, but omit the peas. Serve with baked potatoes or pour over hot biscuits.

Scalloped Potatoes with Dried Beef

7 large potatoes
½ pound (250 g) dried beef
1 large onion, sliced
Crumbs and butter
Whole milk

1. Heat the oven to 375°F/190°C.
2. Pare the potatoes and slice ⅛ inch (¼ cm) thick.
3. Put half the potatoes in a baking dish, then layer the dried beef. Add the onion, then the rest of the potatoes. Sprinkle the crumbs on top, dot with the butter. Pour on the milk, nearly to the top.
4. Bake for 40–50 minutes or until the potatoes are done.

Meat Roll

Baking powder biscuit dough
1 cup (250 ml) chopped cooked meat
Salt and pepper
Onion juice

1. Heat the oven to 350°F/175°C.
2. Make the biscuit dough (see recipe on page 30).
Roll the dough until it is about ¼ inch (½ cm)
thick.
3. Spread the meat over the top of the dough and
sprinkle with the salt, pepper, and onion juice. Roll
up like a jelly roll. Cut slices about ¾ inch (1½ cm)
thick. Place the cut ends down on a greased pan.
4. Bake for about 30 minutes or until well browned.
Serve with tomato sauce (see recipe on page 61),
carrot golden sauce (see recipe page 61), or gravy.

Sweet Potato and Sausage Puff

3–4 sweet potatoes
1 tablespoon butter
1 egg, beaten
1 tablespoon brown sugar
½ teaspoon salt
½ cup (125 ml) cream or milk
¾ cup (185 ml) cooked sausage, minced

1. Boil the sweet potatoes in water for 30–35 minutes or until tender.
2. Heat the oven to 400°F/205°C.
3. Peel the potatoes, and put them through the ricer
or mash them smooth.
4. Add the butter, egg, sugar, salt, and cream. Beat
until light and fluffy. Add the sausage.
5. Pile in a buttered baking dish and bake for 20–25
minutes or until brown on top. Serve at once from
the baking dish.

Salmon Pie

1. Heat the oven to 450°F/230°C.
2. Fill a baking dish with hot creamed salmon or
tuna fish to which has been added cooked carrots,
celery, or other vegetables. Top or dot with small
baking powder biscuits (see recipe on page 30).
3. Bake until the biscuits are done.

Deviled Chicken

2 tablespoons butter
2 tablespoons bread crumbs
2 cups (500 ml) chopped cooked chicken
½ cup (125 ml) cream
2 hard-cooked eggs
Chopped parsley

1. Heat the oven to 400°F/205°C.
2. Melt the butter in a large skillet, add the crumbs, and brown slightly. Add the chicken and cream. Stir until thoroughly heated. Add the eggs that have been put through the potato ricer.
3. Put into a baking dish, sprinkle with the chopped parsley, and brown in the oven.

Scalloped Salmon and Noodles

Serves 10, fine for a club dinner

1 package noodles, 6 ounces (168 g)
⅓ cup (80 ml) butter
⅓ cup (80 ml) flour
3 cups (750 ml) milk
1 teaspoon salt
¼ teaspoon pepper
4 eggs
1 can pink or red salmon, 1 pound (½ kg)
1 cup (250 ml) crumbs
¼ cup (60 ml) butter for crumbs

1. Heat the oven to 375°F/190°C.
2. Cook the noodles in boiling salted water until tender, drain.
3. Make a white sauce of the butter, flour, milk, and seasonings.
4. Beat the eggs slightly and add to the sauce.
5. Divide the salmon in small pieces and add to the egg sauce.
6. Alternate the salmon mixture in layers with the noodles in a buttered baking dish. Cover the top with buttered crumbs.
7. Bake for 25–30 minutes or until heated through and the crumbs are brown.

Adding Glamour to Your Meals

by Theresa Walther Fort

Believe it or not, the American public likes glamour wherever it finds it. Even in tearooms.

If the tearoom has rich furnishings, soft lights and music, and pretty maids in costume, people flock there to absorb "atmosphere" as well as to enjoy the food. But if, as in our case, meals are served in a roomy, old house, in a simply furnished dining room, where a view from wide windows provides our only atmosphere, we must serve the glamour with our food.

The public is not hard to please if food of first quality is well cooked and seasoned and attractively served, if hot dishes are served piping hot and cold dishes thoroughly chilled. The secret lies in planning well-balanced meals with a weather eye out for color combinations. Most people feast first of all with their eyes.

If a party of women orders a plate luncheon of creamed chicken, mashed potatoes, and baking powder biscuits, with the usual salad and dessert, a sprig of green parsley will add color to the plate. But this is not enough—we want a gay touch—so our bis-cuits are cut with a doughnut cutter and served on the creamed chicken, and the hole in the center filled with bright red jelly. Presto—we have our touch. Later several of these women are guests in our dining room again, their hostess having ordered the same menu of creamed chicken and biscuits.

Somehow we must serve this food differently, making it even more attractive if possible. We cut our potatoes into tiny balls and, after boiling gently, pour melted butter over them. The creamed chicken is arranged on the center of the serving plate and a chain of potato balls placed around it. Tiny finger-ring biscuits are dropped onto the creamed chicken. A slice of beet, a section of hard-

cooked egg, a sprig of fresh green parsley, and two strips of carrot give us a garnish for each corner of the square plate.

How much more appetizing is the roast pork surrounded with apple rings, roast beef with strips of carrot or cubes of tomato aspic, roast lamb with individual molds of mint jelly, or veal loaf with slices of green pepper filled with cottage cheese.

We find that sandwiches, salads, and desserts take on a "party air" when cut with fancy cutters or prepared in fancy molds. Cubes made from gelatin desserts of various flavors and color add sparkle to the fruit cocktail, salad, or dessert. Such cubes combined with pears, bananas, pineapple, grapefruit, orange, or white grapes make attractive appetizers.

With a fluted vegetable cutter, such as they sell each year at the county fairs, we frill lemon and cucumber slices and edges of orange, grapefruit, and melon after they are cut in half, also cut fancy shapes from potatoes, beets, and carrots with this cutter. We mold tiny carrots from deep yellow cheese, using sprigs of parsley for stem and leaves. These are served on the salad plate.

Chapter 7

Salads and Salad Dressings

There is an old saying which implies that one has dined well when one has plunged into the depths of a salad bowl. Salads should mean things that are crisp and fresh. We also apply the term salad to rather hearty mixtures of cooked vegetables and meats, fish, or cheese, which are in reality cold supper dishes.

Keep fresh vegetables crisp by storing them in a hydrator or wrapped in a damp cloth in a cool place. To freshen wilted vegetables quickly, put in pan of cold or ice water until crisp, then drain thoroughly. Be sure that vegetables are thoroughly drained before combining or dressing for a salad.

Garnishes may be leaf or head lettuce, celery, cabbage leaves, watercress, parsley, nasturtium leaves, celery leaves or tender curls, or radishes with a bit of green leaf left on. The garnish is usually considered a part of the salad, to be eaten also.

You have fresh foods aplenty for varying the salads of spring, summer, and early fall, but are you familiar with the many different dressings which you can make to accompany them?

You may want to have a plain lettuce salad—then try a Thousand Island dressing or a variation of mayonnaise containing several kinds of finely chopped, spicy pickles or vegetables. Or perhaps you would like a combination of many vegetables which is choicest served with a very simple French dressing, or a fruit salad best blended with a mild cream dressing. It is just as tiresome to make one type do for all salads as it would be to serve potatoes baked once or twice every day.

—*The Farmer's Wife*

Dressings for Every Salad

Any salad dressing contains essential ingredients, as you may have noticed: acid in some form, usually lemon juice or vinegar; fat, which in the uncooked dressing is usually one of the vegetable oils or olive oil, or a combination of olive oil and one of the less expensive oils, also bacon drippings, rendered chicken fat, and drippings from fresh pork or cured ham, which are excellent in the French dressings. Butter is usually used in the cooked dressings, but mild-flavored drippings can also be used in these. An unlimited variety of seasonings may be used, and these somewhat varied from time to time: salt, pepper (white is more attractive than black), paprika, red pepper in very small quantities, onion, mustard, sugar, tabasco sauce, catsup, Worcestershire sauce, and others.

Salad dressings may be grouped on the basis of the form in which the fat appears: either in a temporary or a permanent emulsion, or held in suspension as in the cooked dressings. The methods of combining vary in each of the above cases. The following is a simple classification of salad dressings:

Uncooked Salad Dressings

* Mixtures—bacon fat and acid (usually vinegar).
* Temporary emulsions or French dressings—oil and acid (vinegar or lemon juice) with any desired seasonings. Since in this type of dressing the fat very soon separates out and comes to the top, these should be made just before using, or re-emulsified by shaking or beating when ready to use.
* Permanent emulsions. In these there is something that keeps the fat from separating out.

Cream Dressings

* Thick sour cream and seasonings.
* Thick sweet cream, acid and seasonings.

Mayonnaise

* Egg, oil, acid, and seasonings.

Mock Mayonnaise

* Some emulsifying agent other than egg is used, such as evaporated milk, gelatin, or starch paste. Also we may substitute other fats for the vegetable oil.

Cooked Salad Dressings

* These consist of a liquid (milk or water, and vinegar) thickened with egg or starch or both, which holds the fat in suspension:
* White sauce basis. All the thickening is done with flour or starch.
* Custard basis. All the thickening is done with egg, either yolk or whole egg.
* Combination custard and white sauce basis. Both starch and egg are used.

This is the most usual way of making a cooked dressing.

French Dressing

½ cup (125 ml) oil
¼ cup (60 ml) vinegar
⅓ cup (80 ml) catsup
1 tablespoon grated onion
½ teaspoon salt
1 teaspoon paprika
1½ tablespoons sugar
Juice of ½ lemon

Shake all the ingredients in a small bottle until a thick emulsion is formed.

Variations
Chicken, Pork, or Bacon Fat Dressings: Rendered chicken fat, fresh clarified pork drippings, or mild-flavored bacon drippings may be used in place of the vegetable oil. Use a French dressing made with chicken fat for marinating chicken for a salad.

Cheese Dressings: These are made by adding cheese to a French dressing. Parmesan, Roquefort, and Gorgonzola are especially good, although a more mild cheese, such as American Cheddar can also be used. Grate the cheese if it is a hard cheese, or if too soft to grate, crumble or rub to a paste.

Bacon Dressing: Bits of crisp bacon may be added to any French dressing.

Quick Dressings

These hurry-up dressings are suited to crisp shredded cabbage, lettuce, or greens. Blend the ingredients and pour over the vegetables in a bowl. Toss the vegetables lightly and serve from the bowl.

* Peanut Butter Dressing: ¼ cup (60 ml) peanut butter, ½ cup (125 ml) half-and-half (sweet or sour), juice of 1 lemon or 3 tablespoons vinegar, ¼ teaspoon salt, 1 tablespoon sugar.

* Fruit Juice Dressing: Juice of 1 lemon, juice of 1 orange or ⅓ cup (80 ml) other fruit juice, 1 tablespoon sugar, ¼ teaspoon salt.

* Sour-Sweet Dressing: ¼ cup (60 ml) vinegar, 1½ tablespoons sugar, ½ teaspoon salt, celery seed. Use with cabbage.

* Sour Cream Dressing: 1 cup (250 ml) sour cream, ¼ cup (60 ml) vinegar or lemon juice, ⅓ cup (80 ml) brown sugar, ¼ teaspoon salt.

Thrift Mayonnaise

2 egg yolks or 1 whole egg
½ teaspoon salt
1 teaspoon mustard
⅛ teaspoon cayenne
2 tablespoons lemon juice
2 tablespoons vinegar
1 cup (250 ml) salad oil
⅓ cup (80 ml) flour
1 cup (250 ml) water
1 tablespoon butter

1. Pour the egg yolks, salt, mustard, cayenne, lemon juice, vinegar, and salad oil into a bowl.
2. Then prepare a hot sauce by mixing the flour, water, and butter. Boil the sauce until the flour is well cooked, stirring to keep smooth.
3. Turn the hot mixture into the bowl containing the other ingredients. Beat thoroughly with a rotary egg beater until thick and smooth.

Variations

Russian Dressing: Add 2 tablespoons chili sauce to ½ cup (125 ml) Thrift Mayonnaise.
Thousand Island Dressing: To 1 cup (250 ml) Thrift Mayonnaise add finely chopped: 2 tablespoons green pepper, 1 tablespoon pimento, 2 tablespoons pickles, ½ teaspoon onion, and 1 hard-cooked egg.

Mayonnaise Dressing

Paprika, tabasco sauce, onion, other desired
    seasoning to taste
½–1 teaspoon salt
1 egg yolk or ½ egg
1 cup (250 ml) oil, divided
2 tablespoons vinegar

1. Mix the flavorings and salt in a bowl large enough to accommodate a beater.
2. Add the egg and beat until thick and lemon colored.
3. Add 2 tablespoons of the oil, drop by drop.
4. Then add the vinegar and oil alternately, 1 tablespoon of the oil at a time. Toward the last, the oil may be poured in slowly.
5. Put in a covered glass jar and keep in a cool place.

Note: Eggs used for mayonnaise should not be too fresh. Eggs which have been kept in a cool place for 10 days to 2 weeks are better than newly laid eggs.

Variation

Tartar Sauce: This is used as sauce for fish. Add chopped cucumber pickles and chopped parsley to the Mayonnaise. The characteristic flavor results from tarragon, so add either the chopped or powdered herb or use tarragon vinegar.

Sweet Cream Dressing

1 cup (250 ml) double cream
½ tablespoon sugar
½–1 teaspoon salt
4 tablespoons lemon juice

Beat the cream until stiff. Add the seasonings, and then the lemon juice, drop by drop.

Cooked or Boiled Dressing

½ teaspoon mustard
½ teaspoon salt
¼ teaspoon paprika
3 tablespoons sugar
3 tablespoons flour
2 egg yolks and 1 egg, beaten
⅔ cup (160 ml) water
⅓ cup (80 ml) vinegar
1 cup (250 ml) condensed milk or half-and-half, sweet or sour
2 tablespoons butter

1. Mix all the dry ingredients in a bowl or in the top of a double boiler. Add the eggs, water, and vinegar. Mix well. Add the condensed milk or half-and-half and the butter.
2. Cook in a double boiler or heavy saucepan until thick, stirring constantly. Cool and refrigerate.

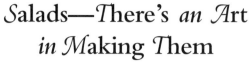

Salads—There's *an* Art *in* Making Them

January 1934

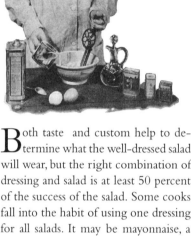

When we first learned to make mayonnaise, that rich, delicious complement to a salad, it was an all morning job.

Now, because we have a better understanding of its real nature, we know that making mayonnaise is simple, sure, and easy.

Both taste and custom help to determine what the well-dressed salad will wear, but the right combination of dressing and salad is at least 50 percent of the success of the salad. Some cooks fall into the habit of using one dressing for all salads. It may be mayonnaise, a boiled dressing, or a French dressing. Whichever it is, she can add infinite variety by varying the dressing on familiar combinations of food and make the family feel that they are getting something brand new.

Most people consider a thick dressing a bit heavy for a dinner salad, when other rich foods are being served. The usual choice is to use a French dressing for a salad to be served at dinner and to use mayonnaise or a boiled dressing when the salad is to be the main dish at an otherwise light meal. Often we use both mayonnaise and French dressing to blend the flavors and to give added zest. In that case, we "marinate" the fruits or vegetables or meats in just enough French dressing to barely coat the ingredients, letting them stand for an hour or longer before meal time. Then add the mayonnaise either as a binder or to garnish the finished salad.

Plain Mayonnaise

Ingredients
1 whole egg or two yolks
3 tablespoons vinegar or lemon juice
½ teaspoon salt
2 tablespoons sugar
1–2 cups (250–500 ml) salad oil

1. With a rotary egg beater combine thoroughly all the ingredients except the oil.
2. Now add 1 tablespoon oil (and this should be measured carefully) and beat it in very, very thoroughly, so that there is no film of oil visible at the edge of the bowl. This takes about a minute, your most important minute in making mayonnaise.
3. When this first tablespoon of oil is incorporated thoroughly, add 2 tablespoons and beat in (your next most important moment), and finally add 3 tablespoons oil and beat in.
4. Now you can pour the oil in, about ¼ cup (60 ml) at a time, but be careful to beat thoroughly after each addition. The mayonnaise thickens as the oil is added. Use enough oil to make it as thick as you like. If it gets too thick, add more vinegar or lemon juice, about a teaspoonful at a time.

Vegetable Salads

Mixed Vegetable Salad Using Cooked Vegetables

1 cup (250 ml) cut asparagus or green peas
1 cup (250 ml) diced carrots or beets
1 cup (250 ml) lima beans or chopped celery
1 cup (250 ml) string beans
⅓ cup (80 ml) sliced green onions or chopped chives
Salt and paprika
Lettuce or celery leaves

1. In a large bowl or container, marinate the vegetables in a French dressing with the salt and paprika to taste.
2. Serve on plates or in a salad bowl with lettuce or celery leaves as a garnish.

Michigan Salad

2 cups (500 ml) shredded or ground carrots
Salt
1 lemon, ground, rind and all
½ cup (125 ml) sugar
6 halves canned peaches or pears, or 6 pineapple or apple slices
Lettuce leaves

1. Put the shredded carrots in a bowl and sprinkle them with a little salt. Combine with the lemon and sugar, and let stand several minutes.
2. Put a generous spoonful of the carrot mixture in the center of the fruit placed on the lettuce. This may be served without the fruit, just on the lettuce or in a bowl.

Delicious Potato Salad

4 cups (1000 ml) cubed, cold potatoes
1 teaspoon salt
Dash of pepper and cayenne
¼ teaspoon paprika
1 tablespoon vinegar
2 tablespoons oil
1 cup (250 ml) chopped celery or shredded
 lettuce
1 cup (250 ml) chopped cucumber and sliced
 radishes
2 tablespoons chopped onion
4 hard-cooked eggs, cut in eighths
2 tablespoons chopped green pepper, pimento, or
 parsley
½ cup (125 ml) chopped sweet pickles
2 cups (500 ml) cooked salad dressing
Shredded lettuce

1. Marinate the cubed potatoes in the seasonings, vinegar, and oil in a large bowl for about 1 hour.
2. Add the other ingredients (except the shredded lettuce) and blend with the dressing. Part of the dressing may be mayonnaise if desired. The salad is improved by standing. The shredded lettuce should not be added until just before serving.

Variations
With Carrots: Add ½–¾ cup shredded carrots to the dressing, omitting some of the other vegetables.
Marinating With Sour Cream: Omit the oil, and instead heat ½ cup (125 ml) sour cream with the vinegar and seasonings. Pour over the potatoes and let stand until cold, before mixing with the other ingredients.

German Potato Salad

5–6 cups (1250–1500 ml) potatoes
Salt to taste
¾ pound (300 g) bacon
2 medium onions, sliced
½ cup (125 ml) vinegar
1 cup (250 ml) water
¾ cup (185 ml) sugar

1. Boil the potatoes with their jackets on. When cool, peel and cube. Salt lightly.
2. Cut the bacon into small pieces, fry, and reserve.

3. Brown the onions in the bacon fat. Add the vinegar, water, and sugar. Allow to boil and add the potatoes.
4. Transfer the mixture to a double boiler, heat thoroughly, and serve hot.

Turkish Salad

1 green pepper, chopped
1 cup (250 ml) shredded cabbage
1 cup (250 ml) chopped celery
1 cup (250 ml) diced apples
½ cup (125 ml) chopped walnuts
Red seedless grapes, cut in halves
Mayonnaise
Lettuce leaves
Rings of green pepper
Celery tips

1. In a large bowl, combine the chopped pepper, cabbage, chopped celery, apples, walnuts, and grapes. Chill thoroughly.
2. Dress with the mayonnaise and serve on the lettuce leaves. Garnish with the rings of green pepper and the celery tips.

Shredded Cabbage or Carrot Salads (Slaws)

With 3 cups (750 ml) shredded cabbage or 2 cups (500 ml) shredded or ground carrots or a combination to the two, add any of the following:
* ½ cup (125 ml) chopped peanuts
* ½ cup (125 ml) grated coconut
* 1 cup (250 ml) shredded pineapple
* 2 oranges, diced, and 4 marshmallows, cut
* ½ cup (125 ml) finely chopped mild onion
* 1 cup (250 ml) diced celery and 2 tablespoons chopped green pepper
* 1 cup (250 ml) banana and ½ cup (125 ml) nuts
* 1 cup (250 ml) apples, cubed, and ½ cup (125 ml) nuts
* ⅔ cup (160 ml) raisins, plumped by standing in hot water

1. These two vegetables—cabbage and carrots—have many interesting possibilities alone or in combination, or with any of the ingredients above. A fine shredder is best for carrots. Cabbage may be cut on a slaw cutter or shredder, or by hand.
2. Use your favorite dressing.

Salads Will Appeal

by Mabel K. Ray

Much is to be said for salads.

They give us an excellent way to include in the diet the raw foods which are needed daily; they are appetizing; they are economical; they give variety to the diet and they can be used for almost every occasion.

Raw foods, both fruits and vegetables, are needed by the body to provide minerals, vitamins, and roughage. We depend upon them especially to furnish vitamin C, since cooked foods, except tomatoes, contain very little of that.

Salads are appetizing when properly made, not only because of their flavor but because of the color or combination of colors they add to the menu.

From the economy standpoint, salads save money. Small amounts of leftovers which otherwise might find their way into the garbage may be combined into a tasty salad.

There is no end to the variety possible in salads. One might easily have a new combination every day for several years, ranging all up and down the scale of raw and canned vegetables, fruits and meats, fish, gelatin salads, and such.

Within reach of every homemaker may be found salads for every occasion. There are dinner salads which are usu-

ally kept simple, light, and tart in nature. Examples of these are green leafy vegetables, a combination of vegetables or fruits, or a tart gelatin salad. Luncheon or supper salads are of the main dish type and quite substantial. Dessert and party salads consist usually of fruit combinations, molded or frozen.

Rules for Salad Making

With a few rules, and with practice, anyone can serve simple, attractive salads. Here are the rules:

Have all the ingredients cold and the salad greens crisp and dry. Salad greens are crisped by letting them stand in cold water 20 to 30 minutes. For greens such as head lettuce and celery, cut the stem end of the plant off fresh, put in cold water and allow to soak the water up. Dry the leaves of the greens on a clean towel or hang in a wire basket and let drain. To keep salad greens crisp for a day or two, put in a damp cloth or bag and place in a well-covered can in a cool place.

Have you had trouble in breaking the leaves of lettuce when taking from the head? If so, cut out the heart and let water from the faucet part the leaves. To keep salads crisp, do not put salad dressing on until just before serving, or pass the dressing at the table. Exceptions are potato and meat salads.

Have materials in salads uniform in size and shape and in well defined pieces. In other words, the one eating it should be able to distinguish what was used in the mixture.

Only ingredients that go together well as to color and flavor should be combined.

Always serve salad over a bed of leaves unless it is a green leafy salad. The bed of leaves may be shredded or whole. Shredded cabbage is excellent to use in this way in the winter and before the spring greens are ready. The garnish should remain within the center of the plate. A salad should be peaked up, not flattened out.

Marinate and drain meat and fish salads and some vegetable salads before serving. To marinate, put French salad dressing over materials and let stand one hour.

Boil home-canned vegetables used in a salad for 10 minutes and chill before using, to avoid chance of food poisoning.

Drain well all canned vegetables and fruits before using in salads. A watery salad is unappetizing.

Never repeat a vegetable or fruit in a salad that will be used in any other way in the meal.

Salad dressing should be chosen according to the characteristics of the salad served. The most common dressings are boiled, French, and mayonnaise. Many variations of these are made. Boiled dressings may be used with any salad combination, French on salad greens and raw vegetables, acid fruits, or fish and cheese salads, while mayonnaise may be used on vegetables, meat and fish when a heavier and richer salad is desired, or with fruit salads when diluted with whipped or thick cream.

Fruit Salads

Waldorf Salad

2 cups (500 ml) diced apple
1 tablespoon lemon juice
1 cup (250 ml) diced celery
½ cup (125 ml) chopped walnuts
Cooked dressing
Whipped cream
Powdered sugar (optional)

1. To prevent discoloration, sprinkle the diced apples with the lemon juice or mix immediately with the cooked dressing (see recipe on page 111). Add the celery and walnuts.
2. Add the whipped cream to the cooked dressing and blend with the apple mixture. Powdered sugar may be added to the cooked dressing if desired.

Variations

With Dates: Substitute ½ cup (125 ml) cut dates for the celery in recipe, or dates for the nuts.
With Bananas: Substitute diced banana for part of the celery.

Stuffed Tomato Salad

1. Allow a whole peeled and chilled tomato for each serving. Cut nearly through each tomato 3 times to make 6 sections, so the tomato can then be spread apart, flowerlike.
2. Fill the centers with one of the following:
* Deviled egg half
* Cottage cheese, plain, or mixed with cucumber or nuts
* Egg salad mixture
* Chicken, fish, or meat salad
* Mixed vegetable salad
* Cabbage salad combinations

Molded Salads

Molded Cottage Cheese Salad

1 package lemon- or lime-flavored gelatin, 3 ounces (85 g)
1 cup (250 ml) warm or hot water
1 cup (250 ml) seasoned cottage cheese, sieved
½ cup (125 ml) shredded canned pineapple

1. In a mixing bowl, dissolve the gelatin in the water, cool.
2. Add the cottage cheese and the pineapple.
3. Mold and chill.

Custard Salad

¼ cup (60 ml) cream
4 egg yolks
⅛ teaspoon salt
Juice of 1 lemon
3 packages lemon-flavored gelatin, 3 ounces (85 g)
1 cup (250 ml) warm or hot water
½ pint (250 ml) cream, whipped
½ pound (250 g) marshmallows
1 can sliced pineapple, 20 ounces (567 g)
1 cup (250 ml) chopped nuts
Whipped cream for garnish
Boiled salad dressing

1. In a heavy saucepan, boil the ¼ cup (60 ml) cream. Add the beaten yolks, salt, and lemon juice to make a boiled custard. Cool.
2. In a mixing bowl, dissolve the gelatin in the water and, when it begins to congeal, beat.
3. To the gelatin, add the whipped cream, marshmallows, pineapple, and nuts. Add the boiled custard.
4. Mold and chill. Serve with the whipped cream and boiled salad dressing, or with the whipped cream alone as a dessert.

Perfection Salad

2 tablespoons granulated gelatin
½ cup (125 ml) cold water
1½ cups (375 ml) boiling water
½ cup (125 ml) vinegar
Juice of 1 lemon
½ cup (125 ml) sugar
1 teaspoon salt
2 cups (500 ml) finely shredded cabbage
1 cup (250 ml) finely chopped celery celery
¼ cup (60 ml) pimentos or chopped stuffed olives or relish

1. In a mixing bowl, soak the gelatin in the cold water until soft. Add the boiling water and stir until the gelatin is dissolved. Add the vinegar, lemon juice, sugar, and salt. Cool.
2. When the mixture thickens, add the vegetables. Mold and chill.

Note: Instead of the plain gelatin, prepared aspic may be used. Follow the directions on the package.

Variation

With Apple: Use 1 cup (250 ml) cabbage, 1 cup (250 ml) grated raw carrots, 1 cup (250 ml) diced apples, and ½ cup (125 ml) chopped nuts in place of the other vegetables.

Tomato Jelly or Tomato Aspic

2 tablespoons granulated gelatin
½ cup (125 ml) cold water
1 can tomatoes, 14½ ounces (411 g)
1 slice onion
3 cloves
2 peppercorns
¼ bay leaf
1 teaspoon salt
1 tablespoon sugar
2 tablespoons lemon juice
Lettuce leaves or cabbage slaw
Mayonnaise or cooked dressing

1. Soak the gelatin in the cold water.
2. Cook the tomatoes and seasonings (all but the lemon juice) for 5–10 minutes. Strain.
3. Pour 2 cups (500 ml) of this hot tomato purée

over the softened gelatin. Add the lemon juice.

4. Pour into wet molds to set. Unmold over the lettuce leaves or cabbage slaw. Top with the mayonnaise or cooked dressing.

Molded Cucumber Salad

1 package aspic or mint-flavored gelatin, 3 ounces (85 g)

1 cup (250 ml) hot water

⅛ teaspoon salt

2 tablespoons vinegar or lemon

1 cup (250 ml) grated cucumber

1. In a mixing bowl, dissolve the gelatin in the hot water. Add the salt and vinegar.
2. When the liquid is cool, add the cucumber.
3. Set in a cool place to thicken.

Molded Cranberry Salad

1 quart (1 l) cranberries

2 whole oranges

2 cups (500 ml) sugar

½ cup (125 ml) hot water

2 tablespoons gelatin

½ cup (125 ml) cold water

1 cup (250 ml) nuts

1 cup (250 ml) celery

1. Grind the cranberries and oranges.
2. Put the fruit in a saucepan and add the sugar and hot water. Boil 2 minutes.
3. Add the gelatin dissolved in the cold water. Cool.
4. Add the nuts and celery. Mold and chill.

Variation

With More Fruit: 1 cup (250 ml) green grapes or 1 cup (250 ml) chopped apple may be substituted for the celery.

Ginger Ale Salad

1 package lime-flavored gelatin, 3 ounces (85 g)
1 cup (250 ml) boiling water
1 cup (250 ml) ginger ale
½ cup (125 ml) green cherries
½ cup (125 ml) red cherries
½ cup (125 ml) grated canned pineapple
½ cup (125 ml) chopped nut meats

1. In a mixing bowl, dissolve the gelatin in the boiling water.
2. Cool and add the ginger ale.
3. Chill until it begins to gel and then add the fruit and nuts. Mold and chill.

Orange Celery Salad

1 package orange-flavored gelatin, 3 ounces (85 g)
1 cup (250 ml) boiling water
1 cup (250 ml) orange juice
1 teaspoon vinegar
2 oranges, diced
1 cup (250 ml) diced celery

1. In a mixing bowl, dissolve the gelatin in the hot water.
2. Add the orange juice and vinegar. Chill.
3. When slightly thickened, fold in the oranges and celery. Mold and chill.

Molded Grapefruit Salad

2 tablespoons gelatin
¼ cup (60 ml) cold water
½ cup (125 ml) boiling water
1 cup (250 ml) sugar
3 tablespoons lemon juice
3 cups (750 ml) grapefruit, pulp and juice
½ cup (125 ml) chopped walnuts
Lettuce leaves
Mayonnaise dressing

1. Soak the gelatin in the cold water in a mixing bowl for 5 minutes. Dissolve in the boiling water, add the sugar, cool.
2. Add the lemon juice, grapefruit juice and pulp, and walnuts. Let stand until the mixture begins to thicken.
3. Mix well and turn into a mold. Chill. Serve on the crisp lettuce with the mayonnaise dressing.

Spiced Pear Gelatin

1 cup (250 ml) sugar
3 cups (750 ml) boiling water
⅓ cup (80 ml) vinegar
2 cinnamon sticks
12 whole cloves
¼ teaspoon salt
10 canned pears
2 tablespoons gelatin
4 tablespoons cold water
Lettuce leaves
Salad dressing

1. In a saucepan, mix the sugar, boiling water, vinegar, spices, and salt. Add the pears, cover, and simmer for 15 minutes.
2. Remove the pears and strain the juice, reserving it.
3. In a mixing bowl, soak the gelatin in the cold water for 5 minutes.
4. Reheat the juice and add the gelatin. Stir until the gelatin is dissolved. Cool.
5. Place the pears in a mold and fill with the gelatin. Chill. Unmold on the lettuce, and top with a salad dressing.

Main Dish Salads

Molded Salmon or Tuna

2 tablespoons gelatin
¼ cup (60 ml) cold water
¼ cup (60 ml) lemon juice or vinegar
1 cup (250 ml) hot, cooked dressing
2 cups (500 ml) flaked salmon or tuna
2 tablespoons chopped pickles
Cabbage slaw or vegetable salad
Mayonnaise
Pickles for garnish

1. In a mixing bowl, soften the gelatin in the cold water and lemon juice.
2. Add the hot, cooked dressing, salmon or tuna, and pickles.
3. Mold and chill. Serve with the cabbage slaw or fresh shredded vegetable salad, garnished with the mayonnaise and more pickles.

Deviled Eggs

4 hard-cooked eggs
¼ teaspoon salt
½ teaspoon prepared mustard
⅛ teaspoon pepper
1 teaspoon vinegar
2 teaspoons mayonnaise or melted butter
Paprika
Lettuce leaves

1. When the eggs are cold, remove the shells and cut each in two, lengthwise.
2. Remove the yolks and set the whites aside. Mash the yolks smooth and mix thoroughly with the salt, mustard, pepper, vinegar, and mayonnaise.
3. Roll the yolk mixture into balls the size of the original yolk. Place a ball in each half white of the eggs.
4. Add a dash of paprika and serve on a bed of crisp lettuce.

Chicken Aspic Salad

3 tablespoons gelatin
½ cup (125 ml) cold water
2 tablespoons chopped parsley
2 tablespoons chopped onion
¼ cup (60 ml) celery leaves
1 quart chicken broth
1 tablespoon lemon juice
2 cups (500 ml) cooked diced chicken
1 cup (250 ml) chopped celery
¼ cup (60 ml) cooked diced carrots
½ cup (125 ml) cooked green peas
¼ cup (60 ml) chopped green pepper
¼ cup (60 ml) chopped pimento
Lettuce leaves
Parsley for garnish
Mayonnaise

1. In a small bowl, soak the gelatin in the cold water.
2. In a large saucepan, simmer the parsley, onion, and celery leaves in the chicken broth for 20 minutes. Add the gelatin. Strain into a large bowl and cool.
3. When the mixture begins to set, add the lemon juice, chicken, and chopped and diced vegetables.
4. Pour into a large or individual molds and chill thoroughly. Unmold and garnish with the lettuce, parsley, and mayonnaise.

Chapter 8

Desserts
and Candies

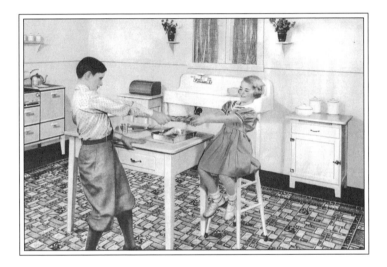

If there are young people in the home, a few afternoons or evenings ought to be
spent by them in making the Christmas candy. For homemade candy is not only
far more pure and more wholesome than most inexpensive candy that is found in
the shops, but it may easily be quite as good as the most costly which is sold there.
When one remembers that cheap candy is often a combination of saccharin, which
tastes like sugar but is a dangerous drug, cornstarch, coal tar dyes, glue and tallow,
they hesitate to give it to the children.

On the other hand, a few pounds of sugar, a little flavoring, milk and butter,
with such raisins, shredded coconut and shelled nuts as the pantry affords may be
turned by the exercise of a little heat and patience into delicious sweets which will
harm no one.

If children or young folks do their own candy making, the house mother should
have it agreed that they wash their sticky cooking utensils and leave the kitchen in
order when they have finished.

Gelatin Desserts

Gelatin desserts are classed as:
* Plain or Fruit Gelatin: Fruit is molded in gelatin or served with it.
* Sponge or Snow: Gelatin mixture is whipped as it thickens until spongy, and usually egg whites are folded in.
* Bavarian Cream: Whipped cream is folded in as the gelatin mixture thickens.

Jellied Prunes

1 package lemon-flavored gelatin, 3 ounces (85 g)
1 cup (250 ml) boiling water
1 cup (250 ml) unsweetened prune juice
1 cup (250 ml) cooked prune halves
Grated rind of ¼ orange

1. Dissolve the gelatin in the boiling water in a mixing bowl. Add the prune juice.
2. When cool, add the prunes and orange rind. Mold and chill.

Lemon Sponge Snow Pudding

1 tablespoon gelatin
¼ cup (60 ml) cold water
1 cup (250 ml) boiling water
¾ cup (185 ml) sugar
¼ cup (60 ml) lemon juice
Few grains salt
2 egg whites

1. In a mixing bowl, soak the gelatin in the cold water and dissolve in the boiling water.
2. Add the sugar, lemon juice, and salt. Set aside to cool, stirring occasionally.
3. When as thick as honey, beat until spongy. Add the whites of the eggs, beaten stiff.
4. Mold and chill. Serve with a custard sauce (see recipe on page 177).

Orange Bavarian Cream

1 tablespoon gelatin
¼ cup (60 ml) cold water
½ cup (125 ml) sugar
1 cup (250 ml) orange juice and pulp
1 tablespoon lemon juice
1 cup (250 ml) whipping cream
Few grains salt

1. Soak the gelatin in the cold water for 5 minutes and dissolve by standing the cup or bowl in hot water.
2. Add the sugar, dissolve. Add the fruit and juice. Cool.
3. When thickened, whip the cream and fold in.
4. Turn into a wet mold and chill.

Variations

Orange-Flavored Gelatin: Dissolve one 3-ounce (85-g) package orange-flavored gelatin in 1 cup (250 ml) warm water, add 1 cup (250 ml) fruit, cool, and proceed as directed above.

Other Fresh Fruit: For the oranges, substitute fresh ripe peaches, apricots, strawberries, or raspberries, first run through a sieve.

Strawberry Ring

Make Strawberry Bavarian Cream (see recipe for Orange Bavarian Cream Variation on page 127) or Strawberry Fruit Gelatin in a ring mold.
Filling for the ring:

1 cup (250 ml) chopped apples
1 tablespoon lemon juice
1 cup (250 ml) whipping cream
2 tablespoons sugar
5–6 marshmallows, cut
½ cup (125 ml) chopped English walnuts

1. Put the chopped apples in a mixing bowl and sprinkle them with the lemon juice.
2. In another bowl, whip the cream and mix in the sugar, marshmallows, and nuts.
3. Combine the apples and cream mixture and fill the center of the ring. Chill.

Chocolate Bavarian

1 tablespoon gelatin
¼ cup (60 ml) cold water
½ cup (125 ml) milk, scalded
2 squares chocolate, melted
⅔ cup (160 ml) sugar
Few grains salt
1 pint (500 ml) whipping cream

1. Soak the gelatin in the cold water in a mixing bowl and dissolve in the scalded milk.
2. Add the chocolate, sugar, and salt. Cool.
3. Whip the cream until stiff and fold in as the chocolate mixture stiffens. Chill.

Cream Fig Pudding

1 package lemon-flavored gelatin, 3 ounces (85 g)
1½ cups (375 ml) boiling water
1 cup (250 ml) whipping cream
1 cup (250 ml) chopped dried figs cooked to a
   thick jam with water

1. Dissolve the gelatin in the boiling water in a mixing bowl. When cold and beginning to thicken, whip to the consistency of whipped cream.
2. Whip the cream and fold into the gelatin with the figs. Chill and serve.

Whips and Puddings

Fruit Whip

1 egg white
¼–½ cup (60–125 ml) sugar
1 cup (250 ml) fruit pulp
Fruit pieces, nuts, or cherries

1. Beat the egg white. Add the sugar and fruit pulp and beat together with an egg beater until stiff as whipped cream.
2. Serve uncooked in sherbet glasses. Garnish with the fruit pieces, nuts, or cherries.

Note: If you wish, pile the mixture lightly in a buttered pudding dish and bake in a preheated oven at 350°F/175°C for about 15–20 minutes. Serve cold with or without boiled custard. Fresh, dried, or canned fruits may be used. Apricots, prunes, and peaches are especially popular.

Sour Cream Prune Whip

2 cups (500 ml) cooked prunes
5 tablespoons sugar
½ cup (125 ml) shredded coconut
½ teaspoon lemon extract
1 cup (250 ml) sour whipping cream

1. Remove the pits from the prunes, chop, and beat to a pulp.
2. Add the sugar, coconut, and lemon extract, and mix thoroughly.
3. Whip the cream until stiff (it must not be too sour or bitter). Add the prune mixture in small amounts and mix thoroughly. Chill and serve.

Note: If sour cream is not available, add 1½ tablespoons vinegar or lemon juice to 1 cup (250 ml) sweet cream after it is whipped.

Fig Tapioca

½ cup (125 ml) tapioca
3 cups (750 ml) hot water
1 cup (250 ml) brown sugar
1 cup (250 ml) ground figs
1 teaspoon vanilla
½ cup (125 ml) nuts
Heavy cream
Grated nutmeg

1. Cook the tapioca in the water until clear.
2. Add the sugar and figs and steam or cook over water in a double boiler until the figs are soft.
3. Remove from the heat and add the vanilla and nuts. Serve cold with the cream flavored with the nutmeg.

Norwegian Prune Pudding

½ pound (250 g) prunes
2 cups (500 ml) cold water
1 cup (250 ml) sugar
Cinnamon stick
⅓ cup (80 ml) cornstarch
⅛ teaspoon salt
1½ cups (375 ml) boiling water
1 tablespoon lemon juice
Heavy cream

1. Wash and soak the prunes in the cold water for several hours.
2. Stew the prunes until soft in same water. Drain and remove the stones.
3. Return the prunes to the saucepan and add the sugar, cinnamon, cornstarch, and salt with a little cold water. Slowly add the boiling water. Stir until thickened, cover, and cook for about 10–15 minutes until the raw taste disappears. Remove the stick of cinnamon and add the lemon juice.
4. Mold and chill. Serve with the cream.

Maple Nut Mold

1½ cups (375 ml) brown sugar
7 tablespoons cornstarch
¼ cup (60 ml) cold water
2 cups (500 ml) boiling water
3 egg whites
¼ teaspoon salt
½ teaspoon maple flavoring
½ cup (125 ml) chopped nuts
Custard sauce

1. Mix the sugar and cornstarch and stir into a smooth paste with the cold water. Stir vigorously while adding the boiling water. Cook for 15–20 minutes in a double boiler.
2. Add the salt to the egg whites and beat until stiff.
3. Combine the egg whites with the cornstarch mixture and add the flavoring and nuts.
4. Pour into molds and chill. Unmold and serve with a custard sauce (see recipe on page 177).

Steamed Puddings

Snowballs

½ cup (125 ml) butter
¾ cup (185 ml) sugar
⅔ cup (160 ml) milk or fruit juice and milk
2 cups (500 ml) flour
2 teaspoons baking powder
⅛ teaspoon salt
4 egg whites

1. Cream the butter and sugar in a mixing bowl.
2. Add the liquid alternately with the sifted, dry ingredients.
3. Beat the egg whites until stiff and fold in last.
4. Turn into buttered molds. Steam for about 45 minutes. Serve with a fruit sauce.

Steamed Date Pudding

2 cups (500 ml) fresh, soft bread crumbs
1 package chopped dates, 8 ounces (227 g)
½ cup (125 ml) nuts, chopped
½ teaspoon baking powder
½ teaspoon salt
½ cup (125 ml) brown sugar
2 eggs, well beaten
½ cup (125 ml) warm water
Cream or half-and-half
Sugar and nutmeg to taste

1. Combine the crumbs, dates, nuts, baking powder, and salt in a large mixing bowl.
2. Add the sugar to the beaten eggs and beat, then add the water, and combine thoroughly with first mixture.
3. Pour into a greased mold, cover, and steam for 45 minutes. Serve with the cream or half-and-half flavored with sugar and nutmeg.

English Plum Pudding

½ pound (250 g) suet, chopped fine
½ pound (250 g) raisins, chopped fine
½ pound (250 g) citron, chopped
½ pound (250 g) currants
½ pound (250 g) brown sugar
1 cup (250 ml) flour
1½ cups (375 ml) soft bread crumbs
1 teaspoon baking soda
1 cup (250 ml) cold coffee (liquid)
1 cup (250 ml) sherry flavoring, grape juice, or
  highly flavored fruit juice
1 teaspoon cloves
1 teaspoon nutmeg
½ tablespoon cinnamon
4 eggs, well beaten
Lemon sauce
Hard sauce

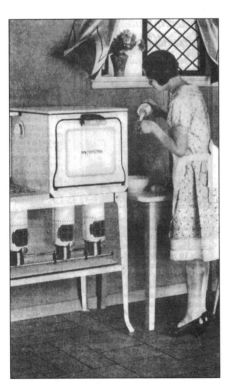

1. Beat all of this well together and steam for 5 hours in large pudding mold or 4 hours in small containers.

2. Serve with a hot lemon sauce topped with a spoonful of Hard Sauce (see recipe on page 177). For a holiday touch, soak cubes of sugar in lemon extract. Put one on top of each serving of pudding and hot sauce. Light the sugar and send into a darkened room, blazing.

Custards and Custard Puddings

Baked Custard

Makes 8–10 cups or 1 large dish

4–6 eggs
½–⅔ cup (125–160 ml) sweetening (white, brown, or maple sugar; honey; maple or caramel syrup)
¼ teaspoon salt
1 quart (1 l) milk, scalded
½ teaspoon vanilla
Nutmeg or cinnamon if desired.

1. Heat the oven to 350°F/175°C.
2. Beat the eggs and add other ingredients as listed, mixing well. Use 4 eggs, if baked as individual custards; 6 eggs, if baked as a large custard. The amount of sweetening depends on taste, but the flavor is much more delicate with the samller amount.
3. Strain into buttered custard cups or a baking dish. Set in a pan of warm water in the oven. Bake for 25–35 minutes for the small cups, 50–60 minutes for a large custard. Test: A silver knife thrust in the center comes out clean. Remove the custards at once from the hot water when they are taken from the oven or they will overcook.

Variations

Surprise Custard: Put a surprise piece of fruit, as a stoned date or pitted prune, or a spoonful of preserve in the bottom of each cup before the custard is poured in.

Rich Custard: Use ½–1 cup (125–250 ml) cream in place of the same amount of milk.

Baked Caramel Custard: Increase the sugar to 1 cup (250 ml). Caramelize the sugar and dissolve in the hot milk. Proceed as in the Baked Custard.

Baked Chocolate Custard: Add 2 squares chocolate or ⅓ cup (80 ml) cocoa and ½ cup (125 ml) water or a chocolate syrup. Melt the chocolate and mix with part of the milk, scalded. With the cocoa, mix it with the water and the custard recipe's sugar, and boil 1 minute. To make a syrup, cook until thick and smooth 1 square chocolate with 2 tablespoons sugar and 2 tablespoons water. Proceed as in the Baked Custard.

Soft Custard: Mix as in the Baked Custard, but cook in a double boiler until it thickens slightly or coats the spoon. Remove from over the hot water and cool. If it starts to curdle, put the container in a pan of cold water and beat vigorously with a wheel beater. Curdling is caused by too high heat. Such a custard is delicious served over fruits such as pineapple or over cakes or puddings.

Floating Island: Same as the Soft Custard. Reserve 2 egg whites. Beat the whites stiff and drop by spoonfuls on boiling water until the islands hold their shape (2 minutes). Place on top of the boiled custard.

Bread or Rice Pudding

1 quart (1 l) milk
2 cups (500 ml) bread, cake, or gingerbread
    crumbs, or cooked rice
3 eggs, beaten
⅓–½ cup (80–125 ml) sugar
½ teaspoon salt
1 teaspoon vanilla or ¼ teaspoon nutmeg
2 tablespoons melted butter
Jelly
2 egg whites
4 tablespoons sugar

1. Heat the oven to 300°F/150°C.
2. Scald the milk; add the crumbs or rice and let stand.
3. Mix as in the Baked Custard, adding the butter last.
4. Bake as a custard. May spread with the jelly and top with a meringue made of the whites of 2 eggs (reserved) and 4 tablespoons sugar. Bake until brown.

Variation

Lemon Bread Pudding With Raisins: Same as the Bread or Rice Pudding, but increase the sugar to ¾ cup (185 ml). Add 1 cup (250 ml) raisins to the crumbs. Mix the grated rind and juice of 1 lemon first with the sugar and eggs, then with the bread and milk mixture. Bake as a custard.

Just Custards

October 1935

When I suggested to the editor that an article on custards should be interesting he asked his usual question, "Why?"

The temptation to say, "Because" was strong, but I thought I'd better prove it by a little experimenting in our Country Kitchen. When the results were tasted and talked over by some of our staff, we were sure that a custard story would be interesting.

Can you make a perfect plain custard—smooth and even, with that delicately fine flavor of eggs and milk brought out, but not obscured, by sugar and flavoring? Here are important things:

Beat the eggs for custard just enough to mix them thoroughly, not until frothy. An exception, of course, is when the eggs are separated as in some special recipes.

If the milk is scalded at the start, the baking time is shortened somewhat. A fairly moderate temperature in baking is best for smooth, tender texture. Set

the custard cups or baking dish on a rack, if possible, (or two or three thicknesses of cloth will do), on the bottom of the pan. Then surround the custard cups or baking dish with hot water. Otherwise the outside edges of a custard are apt to be somewhat porous and cheesy, because of too high a temperature.

It is difficult to get a nicely browned custard unless the oven temperature at the start is quite hot and soon lowered to a very moderate oven. A safe rule, but without a browned top, is to keep the temperature at 350°F/175°C during the entire baking time. Allow 25–30 minutes for cup custards, 50–60 minutes for large custards. A test for doneness is that

a knife blade comes out clean. Remove at once from the hot water when they are taken from the oven or custard will overcook.

Tapioca Cream

3 cups (750 ml) milk, scalded
3 tablespoons quick-cooking tapioca
¼ teaspoon salt
⅓ cup (80 ml) sugar
1 teaspoon vanilla
2 egg yolks, well beaten
2 egg whites, beaten
Sliced fruit, canned, dried, or fresh

1. To the milk, add the tapioca and salt and cook in double boiler according to directions on the package. Stir frequently.
2. Add the sugar and vanilla to the egg yolks. Pour a little of the hot tapioca over the egg mixture and mix.
3. Then return all to the double boiler and cook for 3 minutes longer. Cool slightly, fold in the egg whites.
4. Chill. Pour the tapioca cream over the sliced fruit, such as canned peaches, dates, or bananas.

Note: To vary, use: Brown sugar, maple syrup, or honey in place of the sugar.

Baked Puddings

Date or Fruit Torte

1½ cups (375 ml) chopped dates, dried peaches, or figs
1 cup (250 ml) bread crumbs
1 teaspoon baking powder
½ teaspoon salt
¼ cup (60 ml) chopped nuts
2 eggs, separated
½ cup (125 ml) sugar
½ teaspoon vanilla
Whipped cream or hot pudding sauce

1. Heat the oven to 350°F/175°C.
2. If the dried peaches or dried figs are used, put in a saucepan, cover with water, and boil for 10 minutes. Drain and chop.
3. In a bowl, mix the bread crumbs, baking powder, and salt. Add the fruit and nuts.
4. Beat the egg yolks with the sugar and vanilla.
5. Add the whites, beaten until stiff, and the other ingredients. Mix well.
6. Pour into a greased shallow pan and bake for 30–35 minutes. Serve warm or cold in 2-inch squares with the whipped cream or any hot pudding sauce. Break up cooled torte and coat lightly with whipped cream.

Blitz Torte

Serves 8

Torte Ingredients
½ cup (125 ml) butter
½ cup (125 ml) sugar
4 egg yolks
1 cup (250 ml) all-purpose flour
1 teaspoon baking powder
4 tablespoons milk

Topping Ingredients
4 egg whites
1 cup (250 ml) sugar
Nuts

Filling Ingredients
Ice cream or whipped cream
Berries or other fruit

1. Heat the oven to 350°F/175°C.
2. Cream the butter and ½ cup (125 ml) sugar. Add the egg yolks, beaten lightly. Add the dry ingredients alternately with the milk.
3. Divide the batter between 2 lightly greased layer pans.
4. For the topping, beat the egg whites stiff, add the sugar, and spread on top of the batter before putting it in the oven. Nuts may be sprinkled on top of the meringue.
5. Bake for 25–30 minutes. Lift the meringue to see if the cake is done, before removing from the oven. (The meringue will fall a little.)
6. Use the ice cream or whipped cream between the layers. Cut like a pie and garnish with the berries or fruit.

Cheese Torte

1½ pounds (¾ kg) cottage cheese
8 egg yolks, beaten
1½ cups (375 ml) sugar
3 tablespoons flour
1½ tablespoons butter, creamed
1½ cups (375 ml) thin cream
⅛ teaspoon salt
Rind and juice of 1 lemon
8 egg whites, beaten

1. Heat the oven to 350°F/175°C.
2. Run the cottage cheese through a sieve.
3. Beat the yolks with the sugar and mix with the flour and soft butter. Add the rest of the ingredients, folding in the beaten egg whites last.
4. Bake in a greased baking pan dusted with fine bread crumbs for 45 minutes.

She Sells Fruitcake

December 1936

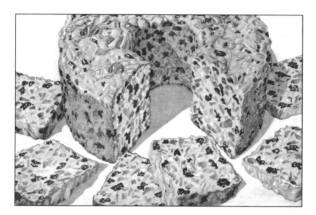

One day five years ago, Mrs. Theresa Walther Fort, a good-looking, happy young woman, walked into a grocery store in Cambridge, Illinois, with 30 pounds of fruitcake.

The storekeeper disposed of only twenty-two for her, but word of Mrs. Fort's fruitcakes spread and kept spreading. Popularity of these dollar-a-pound cakes increased until she sold 500 pounds last year and expects to market 700 pounds this year. Her cakes go to 30 states.

The story really starts 15 years ago, when circumstances forced Mrs. Fort to find a means of support for herself and baby. She decided to take a position as a housekeeper on a farm rather than stay in the city in stenographic work. Resourceful and a good manager, she made party favors in spare time and was forever experimenting with some special dish for community suppers and socials. She started a sideline of fruitcakes for sale because she liked to cook and her neighbors told her that she did it ex-

ceptionally well.

Now she has as a right hand assistant a strapping son who is a high school senior. Last summer Mrs. Fort and Richard moved into Geneseo where they have taken over a big, old-fashioned house to start them in the tearoom business. There is a growing demand for her Sunday dinners and parties, but the fruitcake business is the real story and here it is.

As Mrs. Fort Tells It

We start planning in the spring for our Thanksgiving and Christmas fruitcake business. About May first, we pack 36 dozen fresh eggs in water glass, buying them for about half what they would cost us in the fall. Then during the summer months we make strawberry jams, jellies, apple butter, and grape juice, which are a few of the "additions" we put into the foundation recipe.

About the first of October, we estimate how many pounds of cake we will make and get prices on ingredients in quantity. One evening in the early fall is spent cutting brown paper and heavy waxed paper to fit our various-sized cake tins. Having these papers ready for lining the tins saves considerable delay later.

As soon as the fresh crop of fruits and nuts arrive, we start our baking. Our recipe makes 25 pounds of cake in one mixing, and we have worked out a system for making a hundred or more pounds each week.

The first step is to measure flour, spices, sugar, etc., for four or five batches of cake. Dry ingredients for each individual batch are sifted into a heavy paper sack. Then the fruits are weighed for each batch and piled on separate trays. During leisure hours we cut the fruits. When we are ready to mix a batch of cake, it is a simple matter to assemble the butter, eggs, and liquids and combine them with the other ingredients which are measured and ready.

In spite of the time involved, we cut our fruits by hand, for a food chopper has a tendency to mash them. We take part of the sifted flour and dredge the fruits before cutting. Dates cut best with scissors, but we prefer a paring knife to cut thin slivers of pineapple and citron. Nuts are chopped coarsely in a large wooden bowl.

We have no electric mixers in our home so do all our stirring in a large bowl with wooden spoons. When the

batter is placed in the pans, which have been oiled and lined, first with a brown paper and then a waxed paper, each pan is weighed. An ounce is allowed for each pound for shrinkage in baking. We find it easier to work with pans of uniform size at each baking, thus making all one-pound cakes one day, two-pound sizes the next day, etc.

In some localities our one- and one-half-pound cakes sell best, but other dealers demand the two- and three-pound sizes. We make a five-pound cke on special order. While some of our cakes are oblong, the round ones seem to be the choice for gifts.

After the batter is in the pans, it can be set aside. My cakes sometimes stand 24 hours before baking.

The ideal temperature for small cakes, which should be baked from 2 to 2½ hours is 275°F/135°C. The larger cakes should bake 3 or 4 hours at about 250°F/120°C. We cover our cakes with heavy brown paper while they bake.

When baking fruitcake in a coal range, one can guard against burning by placing about a half-inch of coarse salt over the floor of the oven. An oven thermometer is a great help and costs little.

When the cakes are done we turn them out and remove the papers. After they have cooled thoroughly, they are wrapped separately in waxed paper and packed in covered containers (we use stone jars) to ripen for at least a month.

Fruit Cobbler

1 cup (250 ml) flour
⅓ cup (80 ml) sugar
¼ teaspoon salt
1 teaspoon baking powder
¼ cup (60 ml) milk
1 egg, beaten
1 teaspoon butter, melted
Fresh or canned fruit, sweetened
Lemon, vanilla, or fruit sauce

1. Heat the oven to 400°F/205°C.
2. Sift the dry ingredients. Add the milk, egg, and melted butter. Mix lightly.
3. Arrange the fruit in the bottom of a buttered baking dish and spread with the batter. Bake for 25 minutes or until brown. Serve with lemon, vanilla, or fruit sauce, or cream. As fresh fruit may take longer to cook through than canned fruit, start it cooking before the batter is put on top.

Apple Roly-Poly

3 tablespoons sugar
½ teaspoon cinnamon
Biscuit or shortcake dough
Butter, softened
3–4 sour apples, chopped
Syrup of ½ cup (125 ml) brown sugar and ½ cup (125 ml) water
Foamy sauce or heavy cream

1. Heat the oven to 400°F/205°C.
2. Mix the sugar with the cinnamon and set aside.
3. Make the biscuit or shortcake dough (see recipes on pages 30–31), and pat it into an oblong ½ inch thick. Brush with the soft butter and sprinkle with the sugar and cinnamon mixture. Over this, spread the chopped apples.
3. Roll like a jelly roll. Cut into slices. Place cut sides up in a buttered baking dish about 2 inches deep, leaving space between the slices. Pour the hot syrup over and bake for 35–40 minutes. Serve with the foamy sauce or cream.

Variation

Dumplings: Pat dough ¼ inch thick and cut into individual servings, squares, or triangles. Fill with the apple or other fruit, and pinch together with milk or water. Bake with the smooth sides up, in the syrup.

Brown Betty

4 cups (1000 ml) soft bread crumbs
½ cup (125 ml) butter, melted
4 cups (1000 ml) apples, sliced
Juice of 1 lemon
½ teaspoon grated lemon rind
½ teaspoon cinnamon
1 cup (250 ml) sugar
¾–1 cup (185–250 ml) water or apple juice
Hard sauce or cream

1. Heat the oven to 350°F/175°C.
2. Put the crumbs moistened with the butter in a baking dish, alternately with the apples. Have a top layer of crumbs. Sprinkle each layer with the lemon juice and rind, cinnamon, and sugar. Pour the water or fruit juice over the top.
3. Cover and bake for 1 hour. Uncover for last 15 minutes to brown. Serve hot with Hard Sauce (see recipe on page 177) or cream.

Candies

Temperature and Candy Tests

Use of a reliable candy thermometer is highly recommended. For reference, we include cold water tests. If testing in cold water, first remove the mixture from heat.

Stage	Temperature	Test
Thread	230°F/110°C	Syrup spins a thread from spoon.
Soft ball	236–240°F/113–115°C	In cold water forms a soft ball that can be handled.
Firm ball	245°F/118°C	In cold water forms a firm ball.
Hard ball	250–268°F/120–130°C	In cold water forms a hard ball.
Crack	290–310°F/143–154°C	Hardens at once in cold water, cracks rather than bends when hit on hard surface.
Caramel	350°F/175°C	Syrup turns brown.

Fudge

2 cups (500 ml) sugar
2 squares chocolate or ⅓ cup (80 ml) cocoa
2 tablespoons corn syrup
⅔ cup (160 ml) milk
2 tablespoons butter
1 teaspoon vanilla
Nuts or raisins, if desired

1. Mix the sugar, chocolate, corn syrup, and milk in a heavy saucepan with a wooden spoon. Heat, stirring until the sugar is dissolved. Continue cooking, without much stirring, to the soft ball stage (236°F/113°C on a candy thermometer).
2. Remove from the heat, drop in the butter, allow to stand unstirred until the bottom of the pan is only warm to the touch.
3. Beat until the mixture begins to lose its shiny look, adding the flavoring and nuts before it is ready to turn out.
4. Pour on a greased platter or in a pan. When set, cut in squares.

Note: be careful not to overcook, and let cool before beating. It takes longer and requires more beating, but is much creamier.

Variations

Boston Fudge: Use 1 cup (250 ml) brown sugar, firmly packed, in place of 1 cup (250 ml) white. Use condensed milk.

Sour Cream Fudge: Use 1 cup (250 ml) sour cream in place of the milk. Omit the syrup.

Coffee Cream Fudge

2 cups (500 ml) light brown sugar
½ cup (125 ml) strong cold coffee
¼ cup (60 ml) cream
2 tablespoons butter
⅛ teaspoon salt
½ cup (125 ml) copped pecans or walnuts

1. Mix the sugar, coffee, and cream in a heavy saucepan with a wooden spoon. Cook the mixture slowly without stirring until it boils, then more rapidly until the syrup makes a soft ball in cold water (236°F/113°C on a candy thermometer).
2. Remove from the heat. Add the butter and salt and cool to lukewarm.
3. Beat until thick. Add the nuts.
4. Pour into a buttered pan and cut.

Rich Caramels

2 cups (500 ml) half-and-half, divided
½ cup (125 ml) butter
2 cups (500 ml) sugar
1 cup (250 ml) corn syrup
1 cup (250 ml) chopped nutmeats, if desired
1 teaspoon vanilla

1. In a heavy saucepan, bring 1 cup (250 ml) half-and-half, all the butter, sugar, and corn syrup to a boil, stirring with a wooden spoon.
2. Add the second cup of cream slowly so the boiling does not stop. Cook to a hard ball stage (250°F/120°C on a candy thermometer).
3. Add the vanilla and nuts.
4. Pour into buttered pans. Let stand until firm, then cut.

Pinoche

1½ cups (375 ml) brown sugar
½ cup (125 ml) white sugar
½ cup (125 ml) milk
1 tablespoon butter
¼ teaspoon salt
½ cup (125 ml) chopped nuts
½ teaspoon vanilla

1. Cook the sugars and milk together in a heavy saucepan until it forms a soft ball in cold water (236°F/113°C on a candy thermometer).
2. Add the butter and salt. Stir slightly. Cool quickly over cold water.
3. Add the vanilla and beat until very light in color and creamy in texture.
4. Add the nuts and pour into buttered pans.

Spiced Nuts

1 cup (250 ml) sugar
1 teaspoon salt
½ teaspoon nutmeg
½ teaspoon cloves
2 teaspoons cinnamon
½ cup (125 ml) water
½ pound (250 g) nuts

1. Boil all the ingredients, except the nuts, to the soft ball stage (236°F/113°C on a candy thermometer).
2. Remove from the heat and add the nuts. Stir the mixture until it begins to sugar.
3. Pour quickly onto waxed paper. Cool, and separate the nuts.

Divinity

2 cups (500 ml) sugar
½ cup (125 ml) corn syrup
½ cup (125 ml) water
2 egg whites
Pinch of salt
1 teaspoon vanilla
½ cup (125 ml) nuts, coconut, or fruit

1. Boil the sugar, syrup, and water to the hard ball stage (250°F/120°C on a candy thermometer).
2. Pour over the whites beaten stiff, with the salt. Continue beating until it begins to look dull and gets stiff.
3. Add the flavoring and nuts or fruit.
4. Pour into a deep pan, leaving the top slightly rough. Or drop by spoonfuls on waxed paper. On damp days, it will be necessary to cook the syrup somewhat longer.

Variations

Sea Foam Divinity: Substitute 3 cups (750 ml) light brown sugar for the white and omit the syrup.
Heavenly Hash: Use honey in place of the syrup and 1 teaspoon grated orange rind in place of the vanilla. Add ½ cup (125 ml) shredded coconut and a few chopped and well-drained candied cherries.

Candied Fruit Peel

2½ cups (625 ml) orange or grapefruit peel, cut in strips
cold water
2 cups (500 ml) sugar
1 cup (250 ml) water
Granulated sugar

1. Place the peel in a large saucepan with enough cold water to cover. Bring to the boiling point and boil for about 20 minutes.
2. Drain and repeat once for orange, 2 or 3 times for grapefruit.
3. Make a syrup of the sugar and 1 cup (250 ml) water, boiling until it spins a thread from the spoon (230°F/110°C on a candy thermometer). Add the peel carefully and cook until tender and transparent, rapidly at first, then more slowly. Stir as little as possible.
4. Drain the peel, roll in the granulated sugar, and set to dry in the sun or in a cool oven.

Candied Apple Slices

2 cups (500 ml) sugar
½ cup (125 ml) water
½ cup (125 ml) corn syrup
Few grains salt
4–5 tart apples
Red cinnamon candies or green food coloring and mint flavoring

1. Heat the sugar, water, corn syrup, and salt. Boil until the syrup spins a thread when dropped from the spoon (230°F/110°C on a candy thermometer).
2. Peel and slice 1 apple at a time and drop the pieces in the hot syrup. Cook slowly until the slices are pierced easily and are transparent. During the cooking, add cinnamon candies to color or a little green coloring and mint flavoring.
3. Remove the apple slices and drain. Roll in the granulated sugar and place on a screen or waxed paper to dry.
4. When one apple is finished cooking, prepare another, thinning the syrup with 3–4 tablespoons water each time.
5. Let the slices stand twenty-four hours and roll in sugar. Let stand another day and roll again.

Chapter 9

Cakes, Cookies, and Doughnuts Icings, Fillings, and Dessert Sauces

To be a successful cake maker, learn first of all to make one cake well. From a good, standard recipe many variations are possible.

Start a young daughter who wants to learn to bake on a sour cream cake or the quick plain cake or one of the sponge cakes. Then let her try the small recipe for a butter cake and gradually gain skill in the careful creaming and mixing required with that type. Powdered sugar and butter icings are the simplest; begin there, then try the seven-minute icing. Most difficult to get just right is boiled icing unless a candy thermometer is available.

Fresh cake is delicious served alone as dessert. A generous slice on a plate, served with a fork, makes a dessert to be remembered.

—*The Farmer's Wife*

Cakes

Use all-purpose flour, unless cake flour is called for. Cake flour is a wise choice for fine, rich cakes. Sift or not sift? I always do, and generally before measuring.

Foundation Yellow Cake

A rich basic recipe for a yellow butter cake. From this you can make white, gold, chocolate, burnt-sugar, spice, and other cakes.

Standard Recipe: 3 Layers

3 cups (750 ml) cake flour
¾ teaspoon salt
3 teaspoons baking powder
¾ cup (185 ml) butter
1½ cups (375 ml) sugar
3 eggs
1 cup (250 ml) milk
1 teaspoon vanilla

Smaller Recipe: 2 Layers

2 cups (500 ml) cake flour
½ teaspoon salt
2 teaspoons baking powder
½ cup (125 ml) butter
1 cup (250 ml) sugar
2 eggs
⅔ cup (160 ml) milk
½ teaspoon vanilla

1. Heat the oven to 375°F/190°C.
2. Sift the flour, salt, and baking powder together and set aside.
3. Cream the butter thoroughly in a deep bowl.
4. Add the sugar gradually, beating until the mixture is fluffy and light like whipped cream.
5. Add the eggs, beaten until light.
6. Add the dry ingredients alternately with liquid, beginning and ending with the dry ingredients. Beat thoroughly and add the flavoring.
7. Bake in greased, lightly floured layer pans or a greased, flat loaf pan for 30 minutes.

Variations

*(based on the standard recipe for 3 layers,
except where noted otherwise)*

White Cake: Use 6 egg whites instead of the 3 whole eggs. Beat until stiff, but not dry. Fold in last, lightly but thoroughly.

Lady Baltimore Cake: Make the White Cake in 2 layers (smaller recipe). Make Boiled Frosting (see recipe on page 175) and divide into 2 bowls. To one, add 1 cup (250 ml) chopped nuts and fruit (as raisins, dates, figs), and use to ice the bottom layer. Ice the top and sides with the remaining icing.

Fluffy Spice Cake: Combine 1½ tablespoons mixed spice (a mixture of 4 tablespoons cinnamon, 2 tablespoons nutmeg, and 2 tablespoons allspice or cloves) with 3 tablespoons boiling water. Let stand. Add to the Standard Yellow Cake just before the dry ingredients are added. Use ½ cup (125 ml) strong coffee in place of ½ cup (125 ml) of the milk, if you wish a coffee spice cake.

Spanish Cake: Sift 3 teaspoons cinnamon with the dry ingredients. Ice with Caramel Frosting (see recipe on page 175).

Old-Fashioned Chocolate Cake: Bake a yellow cake in layers and ice with Easy Fudge Icing (see recipe on page 176).

Chocolate Cake: Add 3 squares chocolate, melted, to the standard recipe before the dry ingredients are added. Reduce the butter by 3 tablespoons. Increase the milk by 3 tablespoons.

Gold Cake Or Lord Baltimore Cake: For a rich egg-yolk cake, use 6 yolks instead of the 3 whole eggs in the standard recipe. Beat the yolks until very light with a rotary beater and add to the butter and sugar mixture. Increase the baking powder to 4 teaspoons. Flavor with lemon extract. Ice with Boiled Frosting (see recipe on page 175).

Burnt Sugar Cake: Make a burnt sugar syrup by caramelizing to a golden brown 2 cups (500 ml) white sugar. Add 2 cups (500 ml) hot water and stir until the caramel is dissolved and boil until it makes a thick syrup. Keep in a jar to use as a flavoring for cake, icing, custard, etc. Use 3 tablespoons syrup with the standard recipe. Add to the liquid and combine as usual.

Sour Cream Cake

2 cups (500 ml) cake flour
1 teaspoon baking powder
¾ teaspoon baking soda
½ teaspoon salt
2 eggs
1 cup (250 ml) sugar
1 cup (250 ml) sour cream (thick)
2 tablespoons melted butter
1 teaspoon vanilla

1. Heat the oven to 375°F/190°C.
2. Sift the dry ingredients together and set aside.
3. Beat the eggs in a large mixing bowl. Add the sugar, then the cream, melted butter, and vanilla.
4. Combine the dry and liquid ingredients and beat.
5. Bake for 45 minutes in a greased cake pan or muffin tins. Excellent as a sheet cake or cup cakes with Caramel Frosting (see recipe on page 175), or in 2 layers with Prune Filling (see recipe on page 176).

Variation

Sour Cream Spice Cake: Use 1¼ cups brown sugar in place of the white sugar. Add 3 teaspoons mixed spice (see above recipe for Fluffy Spice Cake) to the dry ingredients.

Sour Cream Cocoa Cake

2½ cups (625 ml) cake flour
2 cups (500 ml) sugar
6 tablespoons cocoa
2 teaspoons baking soda
½ teaspoon salt
½ teaspoon cinnamon
4 eggs
2 cups (500 ml) thick sour cream
1 teaspoon vanilla

1. Heat the oven to 375°F/190°C.
2. Sift the dry ingredients together 3 times and set aside.
3. Beat the eggs until light in a large mixing bowl. Add the cream and vanilla.

4. Add to the dry ingredients and beat well.

5. Grease the cake pans. Bake in 3 layers or as a large sheet cake for about 30 minutes. The recipe is easily divided in half to make 1 sheet cake or 2 small layers.

Devil's Food Cake

2 squares chocolate
2 tablespoons brown sugar
1 cup (250 ml) milk
1 teaspoon salt
1½ cups (375 ml) flour
1 teaspoon baking soda
⅓ cup (80 ml) butter or part other fat
1 cup (250 ml) white sugar
2 whole eggs or 3 yolks and 1 white
1 teaspoon vanilla

1. Heat the oven to 350°F/175°C.

2. Melt the chocolate in a double boiler over hot water or in a heavy saucepan over low heat. Add the brown sugar, milk, and salt. Cook slightly and stir until smooth. Remove and cool.

3. Sift the flour with the baking soda and set aside.

4. Cream the butter in a large mixing bowl and add the sugar gradually until creamy. Then add the eggs, unbeaten, and beat in thoroughly.

5. Add the flour mixture alternately with the chocolate mixture, then the flavoring. Beat.

6. Pour into 2 greased layer pans. Bake for 30 minutes. Frost with Seven-Minute Icing (see recipe on page 174). The whites of 2 eggs may be reserved for the icing if 3 eggs are used.

Applesauce Cake

1 cup (250 ml) sugar
½ cup (125 ml) butter or shortening
1 egg
1 teaspoon cinnamon
½ teaspoon cloves
1 teaspoon baking soda
A little warm water
1 cup (250 ml) unsweetened apple sauce
1 cup (250 ml) raisins
2 cups (500 ml) flour
¼ teaspoon salt

1. Heat the oven to 350°F/175°C.
2. Cream the sugar and butter in a mixing bowl. Add the egg and spices.
3. In another bowl, dissolve the baking soda in a little warm water and add to the applesauce.
4. Combine the 2 mixtures.
5. Dredge the raisins in the flour and add the flour, salt, and raisins.
6. Bake in a greased loaf pan for 45 minutes to 1 hour.

Honey Cake

½ cup (125 ml) shortening
½ cup (125 ml) honey
½ cup (125 ml) sugar
2 eggs, beaten
2 cups (500 ml) flour
3 teaspoons baking powder
¼ teaspoon salt
½ cup (125 ml) milk
2 teaspoons cream

1. Heat the oven to 350°F/175°C.
2. Cream the shortening, honey, and sugar in a large mixing bowl. Add the beaten eggs. Beat the mixture until thoroughly blended.
3. Sift the flour, baking powder, and salt together.
4. Add the dry ingredients alternately with the milk to the honey mixture. Do not beat after all the flour has been added. Simply stir to be sure it is well blended.
5. Add the cream. Stir.
6. Pour into 2 layer cake pans, lined with waxed paper and greased both on the bottom and sides. Bake for about 45 minutes.

Variations

Spice Honey Cake: Add 2 teaspoons mixed spice (see recipe for the Fluffy Spice Cake on page 151) to the honey-butter-sugar mixture.

Nut Honey Cake: Add 1 cup (250 ml) chopped hickory nuts, when the last of the flour is added.

Banana Cake

½ cup (125 ml) butter
1½ cups (375 ml) sugar
2 egg yolks
1 teaspoon soda
4 tablespoons sour cream
2 cups (500 ml) cake flour
½ cup (125 ml) water
1 cup (250 ml) mashed banana
1 teaspoon vanilla

1. Heat the oven to 375°F/190°C.
2. Cream the butter in a large mixing bowl, adding the sugar gradually. Add the egg yolks, well beaten.
3. Mix the soda in the sour cream and add alternately with half the sifted flour. Alternate the water with the remaining flour.
4. Add the mashed banana and vanilla.
5. Pour into a flat, greased pan and bake for 45 minutes to 1 hour.

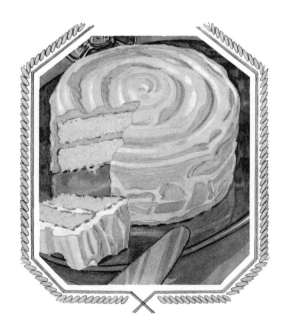

Tomato Soup Cake and Cream Cheese Frosting

Cake Ingredients
½ cup (125 ml) butter
1 cup (250 ml) sugar
2 cups (500 ml) flour
2 teaspoons baking powder
1 teaspoon cinnamon
1 teaspoon cloves
1 teaspoon nutmeg
1 teaspoon salt
1 teaspoon soda
1 can condensed tomato soup, 10¾ ounces
   (305 g)
1 cup (250 ml) chopped nuts
1 cup (250 ml) chopped dates or raisins

Frosting Ingredients
8 ounces (227 g) cream cheese
1½ cups (375 ml) powdered sugar
1 teaspoon vanilla
Milk to moisten

1. Heat the oven to 350°F/175°C.
2. Cream the butter in a large mixing bowl and add the sugar.
3. Sift the flour, baking powder, cinnamon, cloves, nutmeg, and salt and set aside.
4. In a small bowl add the baking soda to the soup.
5. Add the dry ingredients and the liquid alternately to the creamed butter and sugar. Stir in the nuts and dates.
6. Bake for 45 minutes in a greased pan.
7. To make the frosting, beat the cream cheese, powdered sugar, vanilla, and milk together until creamy.

Orange Cake

2 cups (500 ml) sugar
¾ cup (185 ml) butter
4 eggs, separated
1 large orange
¾ cup (185 ml) water
3 cups (750 ml) flour
2 teaspoons baking powder

1. Heat the oven to 375°F/190°C.
2. Cream the sugar and butter together in a large mixing bowl.

3. Whip the yolks of the eggs and add.

4. Add the juice and grated rind of the orange to the water and pour over the mixture.

5. Place the unbeaten egg whites on top of the liquid.

6. Measure the flour after sifting. Add the baking powder and sift again over the egg whites and liquid. Whip all together until fine and smooth.

7. Separate the batter into 2 greased layer cake pans. Bake for approximately 30 minutes.

Nectar Raisin Cake

1 cup (250 ml) raisins
¾ cup (185 ml) raisin water
½ cup (125 ml) shortening (part butter)
¾ cup (185 ml) sugar
1 egg, beaten
1⅔ cups (400 ml) flour
1 teaspoon cinnamon
1 teaspoon allspice
1 teaspoon nutmeg
1 teaspoon baking powder
½ teaspoon salt
½ teaspoon baking soda
½ teaspoon vanilla
1 cup (250 ml) chopped nuts

1. Heat the oven to 375°F/190°C.

2. Put the raisins in 1 cup (250 ml) boiling water in a saucepan and cook for 10 minutes. Drain, saving ¾ cup (185 ml) of this raisin water for the cake.

3. In a large mixing bowl, cream the shortening and sugar well. Add the beaten egg.

4. Sift all dry ingredients except the baking soda.

5. Add the baking soda to the raisin water and add to the creamed mixture alternately with the flour mixture.

6. Add the vanilla and the nuts and raisins that have been floured with a little of the flour.

7. Bake in a greased loaf pan or layer pans for approximately 30 minutes.

Perfect Gingerbread

2 cups (500 ml) flour
½ cup (125 ml) sugar
1½ teaspoons ginger
½ teaspoon cinnamon
2 teaspoons baking powder
½ teaspoon baking soda
¼ teaspoon salt
¾ cup (185 ml) molasses
1 cup (250 ml) sour milk or 1 cup (250 ml) sweet
    milk and 1 tablespoon vinegar
1 egg
¼ cup (60 ml) melted shortening

1. Heat the oven to 350°F/175°C.
2. Put all the dry ingredients in a sifter.
3. Put the wet ingredients in a mixing bowl.
4. Sift in the dry ingredients and beat until smooth.
5. Fill a well-greased and floured shallow pan only half full. Bake for 20–45 minutes, depending on the pan size.

Variations

Apple Gingerbread: Pare, core, and slice several apples. Put in the bottom of a square or oblong pan and sprinkle with sugar. Add a small amount of water and put in the oven to start cooking. When partially cooked, pour the gingerbread batter over the apples and bake. Serve warm with cream.
Marshmallow Gingerbread: While the bread is still warm, split carefully into 2 layers and put 3 dozen large marshmallows between and on top. Put back in a warm oven until soft, puffy, and golden brown.
Banana Gingerbread: While the gingerbread is still warm, cover with sliced bananas and whipped cream.

Very Best Fruitcake

¼ pound (100 g) citron
¼ pound (100 g) lemon peel
¼ pound (100 g) orange peel
½ pound (250 g) candied cherries
½ pound (250 g) nutmeats
½ pound (250 g) dates
½ pound (250 g) candied pineapple
¼ pound (100 g) coconut
½ pound (250 g) raisins
2 cups (500 ml) flour
1 teaspoon allspice
½ teaspoon nutmeg
½ teaspoon cloves
1 teaspoon salt
1 teaspoon baking powder
½ pound (1 cup (250 ml)) shortening
½ cup (125 ml) sugar
⅓ cup (80 ml) honey
3 eggs
6 tablespoons orange juice

1. Shred the citron and the peel. Halve the cherries, nutmeats, and dates. Cut the pineapple in pieces, the size of almonds. Chop the coconut very fine. Dredge the fruit, including the raisins, thoroughly in ¼ cup (60 ml) or more of the flour. Set aside in a large mixing bowl.
2. Heat the oven to 275°F/135°C.
3. Sift the remaining flour with the dry ingredients and set aside.
4. In a large mixing bowl, cream the shortening with the sugar, then add the honey. Stir in the eggs, well beaten.
5. Add the dry ingredients and the orange juice alternately, blending thoroughly.
6. Pour the batter over the floured fruit and mix until all the fruit is well covered.
7. Line oiled baking tins with 3 layers of waxed paper, allowing ½ inch of paper to extend above all sides of the pan.
8. Pour all the batter into pans lightly. Do not flatten.
9. Place a flat pan containing 2 cups (500 ml) water in the bottom of the oven while baking. Bake for 2½–3 hours or until a wooden pick inserted in the center comes out clean.

Sunshine Cake

1 cup (250 ml) cake flour
1 cup (250 ml) sugar
6 large fresh eggs, separated
2 tablespoons water
1 tablespoon lemon juice
½ tablespoon grated lemon rind
½ teaspoon salt
Whipped cream or fruit

1. Heat the oven to 325°F/160°C.
2. Sift the flour and the sugar separately.
3. In a mixing bowl, beat the egg yolks until lemon colored and thick.
4. Add the water, sugar, lemon juice, rind, and salt gradually. Beat until smooth and creamy.
5. Whip the egg whites until light and fold in to the batter.
6. Carefully and lightly sift in the flour ¼ cup (60 ml) at a time, and fold in gently.
7. Bake in an ungreased tube pan for 40–60 minutes. When done, the cake shrinks from the pan and springs back when touched. Invert the pan on cake rack, letting cake hang until cool. Serve with the whipped cream or fruit.

Note: Sunshine, Angel Food, Hot Milk Sponge, and Dutch Cakes are sometimes called "foam cakes." Their batters are made without butter or shortening. For leavening, these cakes depend on air and steam trapped in their well-beaten, foamy egg-rich batters.

Angel Food Cake

1 cup (250 ml) cake flour
1 cup (250 ml) egg whites (approximately 12 eggs)
¼ teaspoon salt
1 tablespoon water
1 teaspoon cream of tartar
1¼ cups sugar
¼ teaspoon almond extract
½ teaspoon lemon extract

1. Heat the oven to 375°F/190°C.
2. Sift the flour 4 times after measuring.
3. Beat the egg whites lightly with a whisk in a

large mixing bowl. Add the salt, water, and cream of tartar when half beaten.

4. When the egg whites will hold their shape, gradually fold in the sugar and then the flour, a tablespoon at a time.

5. Blend in the flavoring.

6. Bake in an ungreased tube pan for 30–35 minutes or until the cake springs back when touched lightly with a finger. Invert on a cake rack and allow to cool in the pan. In serving angel food cake, separate into pieces with two forks rather than cutting with a knife.

Hot Milk Sponge Cake

2 eggs
1 cup (250 ml) sugar
1 cup (250 ml) cake flour
⅓ teaspoon salt
1 teaspoon baking powder
½ cup (125 ml) hot milk
2 tablespoons butter, melted in milk

1. Heat the oven to 350°F/175°C.

2. In a large mixing bowl, beat the eggs about 8 minutes until very thick and lemon colored.

3. Add the sugar ⅓ cup (80 ml) at a time and continue beating.

4. Sift the dry ingredients together, and stir in.

5. Add the hot milk and butter. Blend well.

6. Turn into a deep layer tin lined with waxed paper. Bake for 30 minutes. Invert the pan to cool. This recipe is suitable for upside-down cakes.

Cake by Request

by Mabel K. Ray

The word "cake" may conjure visions of a hundred different cakes to a hundred different people, but when it comes down to facts there are really only two distinct kinds: those made with fat and those made without. In the first class are "yummy" devil's food cakes, plain yellow and white cakes with variations, and pound cakes, while sponge and angel cakes make up the latter.

The cakes made with fat, except pound cake, are leavened by the carbon dioxide produced by the action of the baking powder or the use of sour milk or cream with soda, while the sponge cakes depend for leavening on the air put into the mixture through beating the whites of eggs, sifting the flour, and special care in combining the ingredients.

The Ideal Cake

An ideal cake should be uniform in thickness, light in weight, fine, of even grain, neither moist nor dry, and have a delicate, agreeable flavor and odor.

Shortened cake should have a golden brown, smooth crust with a slightly rounding top, while unshortened cakes should have a lighter brown color and be somewhat rough with either a slightly rounding or flat top.

In cakes made with fat there are two principal ways of combining the ingredients, known as the muffin method and the conventional method. (The muffin method and two conventional methods are described in the recipe for plain cake.)

When one is in a hurry and wishes the cake for immediate use, the muffin method is good to use. A cake made this way is coarser grained and does not retain its freshness as well as do those mixed by the conventional methods.

Even cakes made from the same ingredients, in the same proportions, by the same conventional method vary greatly as to the length of time they keep their freshness. According to Holliday and Noble, "the reason for this happens to be that the quality of staleness is not altogether a matter of dryness (loss of water) but partly a question of distribution among different components of the mixture."

To Make the Ideal Cake

To obtain a cake with ingredients evenly distributed, the following points should be considered: uniform particles of flour and sugar obtained by sifting or use of special flour; a fine baking powder with uniform particles; butter or fat well creamed, and thorough combination of ingredients.

In a plain cake, it is not necessary to beat the yolks and whites separately to get a good result, provided they are beaten into the creamed fat and sugar mixture thoroughly.

In sponge or angel food cakes, the trick is in getting the egg whites combined with the other ingredients without breaking the air bubbles already incorporated. The ingredients must be well mixed, however, or a coarse, uneven texture will result. Folding the sugar and flour into the egg mixture with gentle movements is a requisite.

While good cakes can be made with either cake or bread flour, it is easier to make a good cake with cake flour and one which will stay fresh longer, because the particles of cake flour are finer and contain much less gluten, and that gluten is of a type that helps to make a tenderer product. If the recipe calls for bread flour and you wish to use cake flour, use 1 cup (250 ml) plus 2 tablespoons of cake flour to each cup called for in the recipe. If cake flour was called for and you have bread flour at hand, subtract 2 tablespoons from each cup listed.

A question which comes up often in regard to devil's food or chocolate cake is how to obtain that deep red color. The redness of that type is caused by an excess of soda over the amount needed to neutralize the sour milk or cream which was perhaps used. One-half teaspoonful of soda neutralizes 1 cup (250 ml) of medium sour milk. Recipes in which sweet milk and soda are used, besides baking powder, usually produce a red cake due to the fact that the soda has nothing to neutralize in this case and an alkaline medium is produced.

Three tablespoons of cocoa and ½ tablespoon of butter are equal to one ounce or square of chocolate.

When substituting cream in a recipe in place of liquid and fat, remember: medium cream is about 25 percent butter fat and is equivalent to ¾ cup (185 ml) sweet skim milk, less 1 tablespoon, plus 5 tablespoons fat; heavy cream is about 40 percent butter fat and is equiva-

lent to ½ cup (125 ml) sweet skim milk plus ½ tablespoon, plus 7½ tablespoons fat.

Other Helpful Facts About Cake Baking:

Dredge nuts or fruit in part of required flour to keep them from going to bottom of batter.

Butter is an excellent shortening to use for plain cakes due to its pleasing flavor. For chocolate, spice, or other strongly flavored cakes, other fats are good.

Egg whites beat up to better advantage, both as to time and volume, when the eggs are of room temperature.

When adding dry ingredients alternately with the liquid, begin and end with the dry ingredients in order to keep the fat from separating from the sugar and egg.

Immediately after mixing, pour the cake batter into the pans in which it is to be baked. If this is done, cake made with any type of baking powder may stand a few minutes before baking. Those made with slow-acting baking powder, of course, can stand much longer without ill effects. It is the pouring of the batter after it has stood and the breaking of the gas bubbles already formed that make for failure.

Cakes made with bread flour should be beaten less than cakes made with cake flour since beating develops the gluten and may cause large tunnels.

Dutch Cake

Cake Ingredients
1 egg
1 cup (250 ml) granulated sugar
2 cups (500 ml) flour
1 cup (250 ml) milk
1 teaspoon baking powder
⅛ teaspoon salt

Topping Ingredients
1 cup (250 ml) brown sugar
1½ teaspoons cinnamon
⅓ cup (80 ml) butter

1. Heat the oven to 350°F/175°C.
2. Beat the egg until light in a large mixing bowl. Add the sugar.
3. Add a small amount of the flour, the milk, and then the remainder of dry ingredients.
4. Divide the batter between 2 layer cake tins.
5. To make the topping, mix the sugar and cinnamon. Spread over the layers and dot with the butter.
6. Bake for 25–30 minutes. This cake is excellent with coffee.

Cookies and Doughnuts

Cookies may be crisp or soft, large or small, according to one's wish. Crisp cookies mean that a comparatively small amount of flour is used and a generous amount of fat. To avoid working in excess flour in rolled cookies, chill the dough thoroughly before handling. Less flour is rolled in if you use a canvas cover or towel dusted with flour over your board and a stockinet cover for the rolling pin.

Sour Cream Drop Cookies

¼ cup (60 ml) butter
1¾ cups sugar
2 eggs, beaten
1 cup (250 ml) thick sour cream
3 cups (750 ml) sifted flour
1 teaspoon baking soda
1 teaspoon baking powder
½ teaspoon salt
1 tablespoon grated rind of orange or lemon
Raisins
Sugar

1. Heat the oven to 400°F/205°C.
2. Cream the butter and ½ cup (125 ml) of the sugar in a large mixing bowl.
3. Beat the eggs with the rest of the sugar and the cream and add to the butter mixture.
4. Sift the flour with the baking soda, baking powder, and salt. Add the grated rind, then combine with rest of the ingredients to make a drop batter.
5. Drop on a greased sheet, top with a plump raisin and a sifting of sugar. Bake for 12–15 minutes.

Sour Cream Molasses Cookies

1 cup (250 ml) butter
1 cup (250 ml) brown sugar
1 cup (250 ml) molasses
3 eggs, beaten
1 cup (250 ml) sour cream
2 teaspoons baking soda
1½ teaspoons salt
1½ teaspoons ginger
3 teaspoons cinnamon
6 cups flour (approximately)

1. Heat the oven to 350°F/175°C.
2. Cream the butter in a large mixing bowl. Add the sugar, molasses, eggs well beaten, and sour cream.
3. Mix and sift the baking soda, salt, ginger, cinnamon, and 1 cup (250 ml) flour and add. Then add enough more flour to make a drop batter.
4. Chill several hours, roll out, and cut in rounds. Place on a greased tin and bake for 12–15 minutes. Ice while warm, if desired, with a powdered sugar and cream icing.

Variation

Molasses Creams: If desired, spread the batter, without chilling, in a shallow, greased pan and bake. While still slightly warm, ice with a powdered sugar and cream icing. Leave in the pan until ready to serve, then cut in bars.

Say It with Cookies

There's nothing quite like cookie-baking day. Nothing quite so cheerful in its floury confusion as the cookie-day kitchen, or so compelling as the spicy smell when each pan comes from the oven. Nothing quite so absorbing to the cook as this task which keeps both hands busy and demands one watchful eye on the oven and another on the children making inroads on the freshly baked heap. And nothing quite so festive and Christmasy as a varied assortment of cookies packed as a gift.

Arrange them in orderly rows or groupings on a plate or tray of the sort that Cousin Nellie has been wanting, or in a basket which will please Uncle John, who must always have fruit handy, or in a big cookie jar for the Graysons with their lively, ever-hungry youngsters. Tie up in a shimmery, transparent wrapping, deck with a sprig or two of green, and let everyone peek, if they choose to see just what kinds are waiting to be sampled.

Crunchy peanut cookies or coconut macaroons, rich satisfying frosted nut squares, anise- and honey-flavored chocolate rounds, delectable almond cookies in fancy shapes, crisp sugar stars and diamonds—these are gift goodies surely enough.

There are ways to get around cutting out cookies, unless you want fancy shapes. Then a rich dough is rolled thin on canvas or board. But for plain, round cookies, we learned one good method a few years ago: making the dough in a roll, then chilling, and slicing it into thin rounds. Another method explained in the cookbook for a new vegetable shortening is to place small balls of the dough on the greased tin, then stamp them flat with the bottom of a glass which is covered with a damp cloth. Moisten the cloth as needed by dipping in water and removing excess moisture on a towel. We found that it made uniform, even circles, provided, of course, you made uniformed sized balls. Other cookies are dropped, and an increasingly popular kind is the sort which is spread out in a rectangular shallow pan, to be cut in squares after baking.

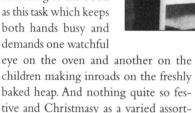

Date Bars

⅔ cup (160 ml) flour
¼ teaspoon salt
½ teaspoon baking powder
2 cups (500 ml) dates sliced
½ cup (125 ml) chopped nuts or 1 cup (250 ml)
  coconut
2 eggs
½ cup (125 ml) granulated sugar
Powdered sugar

1. Heat the oven to 325°F/160°C.
2. Sift the flour, salt, and baking powder in a mixing bowl.
3. Add the dates and nuts, and mix.
4. In another bowl, beat the eggs until very light. Add the granulated sugar gradually and beat. (If the eggs are small, 2–3 tablespoons water may be added.)
5. Add the egg mixture to the flour and fruit mixture.
6. Spread thin in well-oiled pans, and bake for about 40 minutes. Remove from pan after it has been out of oven for a few minutes and cut in strips. Roll in the powdered sugar and store in a tightly covered can or box.

Crispy Sugar Cookies

4 cups (1000 ml) flour
3 teaspoons baking powder
½ teaspoon nutmeg
1 teaspoon salt
1 cup (250 ml) butter
2 cups (500 ml) sugar
2 eggs, well beaten
Grated rind of 1 lemon
¼ cup (60 ml) sweet cream

1. Heat the oven to 400°F/205°C.
2. Sift the flour with the baking powder, nutmeg, and salt.
3. Cream the butter thoroughly in a mixing bowl. Add the sugar gradually and cream together until light and fluffy.
4. Add the eggs, lemon rind, and cream, and beat well.
5. Add the flour, part at a time. If the dough is not too warm, it will handle with the amount of flour in the recipe. The cookies will not be crisp if too much flour is used.
6. Roll into a thick sheet on very lightly floured board, cloth, or canvas. Dredge with sugar and roll over lightly. Cut with a floured cookie cutter.
7. Bake on a greased cookie sheet for 8–10 minutes or until a delicate brown.

Variations

With Sour Cream: Use only 1 teaspoon baking powder and add ½ teaspoon baking soda if sour cream is used in place of the sweet cream.

Filled Cookies: Cut the sugar cookies in 3-inch rounds and place about ½ teaspoon filling on half the cookie. Fold over, press the edges together. Filling: Mix together 2 tablespoons flour and ½ cup (125 ml) sugar. Add ½ cup (125 ml) boiling water. Cook until thick. Add 2 cups (500 ml) chopped dates or raisins, ½ cup (125 ml) chopped nuts, and 2 tablespoons lemon juice.

Coconut Flake Macaroons

Makes 30

2 egg whites
¼ teaspoon salt
1 cup (250 ml) sugar
1 cup (250 ml) shredded coconut
2 cups (500 ml) crisp corn flakes
½ teaspoon vanilla
1 tablespoon flour

1. Heat the oven to 325°F/160°C.
2. Beat the egg whites with the salt in a mixing bowl.
3. Add the sugar gradually, then the coconut, corn flakes, and vanilla. Mix well and then add the flour.
4. Drop by spoonfuls onto buttered sheets. Bake about 20 minutes.

Variation

Popcorn Macaroons: Instead of the corn flakes, use wheat or rice flakes or puffed wheat or rice.

Chocolate Brownies

1 cup (250 ml) sugar
¼ cup (60 ml) melted butter
2 eggs, unbeaten
2 squares chocolate
½ teaspoon vanilla
½ cup (125 ml) flour
½ cup (125 ml) chopped nutmeats
¼ teaspoon salt

1. Heat the oven to 325°F/160°C.
2. Mix the ingredients in the order given.
3. Grease and line a square pan with waxed paper. Spread the mixture evenly in the pan. Bake for 25–30 minutes. Turn out and cut in squares while still warm. The brownies will be hard when taken from the oven, but will soften if stored in a can for a few hours.

Delicious Doughnuts

¾ cup (185 ml) sour cream
¼ cup (60 ml) sour milk
1 cup (250 ml) sugar
3 eggs, beaten
3½ cups flour
1 teaspoon soda
1 teaspoon baking powder
½ teaspoon nutmeg
½ teaspoon salt
Fat for frying

1. To the sour cream and milk, add the sugar and let dissolve.
2. Add the eggs, then the sifted dry ingredients to make a soft dough. A small amount of additional flour may be needed.
3. Roll out to ¼-inch (½-cm) thickness and cut. Let stand 30 minutes to dry on the outside.
4. Fry in the deep fat heated to 365°F/185°C (will brown a cube of bread in 60 seconds). Fry enough to make 1 layer on top of the fat and turn just once during frying. Remove, drain on unglazed paper. Dust with sugar, if desired.

When It's Doughnut Day

by Miriam J. Williams, November 1933

The day we were deep-fat frying in the Country Kitchen, an unusual number of callers dropped in. But since we are always glad for opinions about our products, I wasn't sorry that our frequently opened door let out the odorous message that it was doughnut day. Our visitors saw and tasted an interesting assortment of doughnuts and fritters that were made according to readers' recipes. I am quite certain that many country and town kitchens would be glad to hear about them.

How We Make Doughnuts in the Country Kitchen

For frying, we heated 3 pounds (1½ kg) of lard in a deep kettle. We chose lard as a typical farm fat. Other vegetable types of fats and oils are very satisfactory, however, and, there is little difference in price this year.

The fat was heated to 360°F/180°C, or hot enough to brown a cube of bread in 50 seconds. Each lot of food cooled the fat, of course, so we were careful to see that the heat was steady during frying and that the initial temperature of each frying was kept the same.

We used a deep-fat frying thermometer which hooked over the edge of the kettle with the bulb immersed in the fat.

Temperature of fat is important, for a too cool fat means that food becomes grease-soaked, while a too hot fat browns the outside of a doughnut or fritter before the inside is thoroughly cooked. Overheating also results in a breaking down of the fat, a fact too of-

ten spread about on deep-fat frying days by an acrid, unpleasant odor. We are told, too, to keep flames from creeping onto the sides of a fat kettle, or the fat near the edge will become overheated.

In mixing doughs for deep-fat frying, we took pains to keep the dough fairly soft, or we knew the result would be bready, dry doughnuts. Just stiff enough to handle is a good general rule. It is helpful to allow the outside of the cut doughnut to dry slightly before frying, as a dry surface is less likely to become grease-soaked. We used a pastry canvas on our bread board, and a white stocking over the rolling pin to help keep from using an excess of flour in rolling out the dough.

We found it wise to drop in just enough doughnuts or fritters at one time so that they would cover the surface of the fat when they would rise. If there was any tendency for them to crack, they were turned several times during frying until the right shade of browness was secured.

Unglazed paper on a flat pan was close by so that each piece was removed and drained, excess fat was absorbed by this paper.

As you are frying, free the fat of small particles of food which will escape, for if they remain they become too brown and cause the fat to deteriorate.

Regulation doughnuts, knots, squares, cruller-twists, or just drops of dough are all possible from the same dough if you wish to have variety. Avoid any piece which is too thick for quick cooking, or the center will be doughy.

Icings, Fillings, and Dessert Sauces

Seven-Minute Icing

1 cup (250 ml) sugar
1 egg white
3 tablespoons water
Few grains salt
½ teaspoon vanilla

1. Put all the ingredients except the vanilla in the top of a double boiler. Cook over boiling water for 7–10 minutes, beating all the while with a rotary beater. When ready to remove from the stove, the icing will be thick and almost ready to spread.
2. Add the vanilla, beat until cool and ready to spread. Double the recipe for all but a small cake.

Variations

Chocolate: Melt 1 square chocolate in the double boiler, add the other ingredients and proceed as above.

Marshmallow: Add 8 marshmallows, cut in pieces, when the icing is partly cooled to make a fluffier icing.

Butter Icing

⅓ cup (80 ml) butter
2 cups (500 ml) powdered sugar
1–2 tablespoons cream
½ teaspoon vanilla

1. Soften the butter by creaming in a mixing bowl and add the sugar gradually.
2. Add enough cream to make the icing spread and add the flavoring. Butter icing may be put through a pastry tube.

Variations

Coffee Butter Icing: Use strong, hot coffee in place of the cream.

Orange Butter Icing: Use orange juice in place of the cream to moisten and 2 teaspoons grated orange rind for the flavoring.

Boiled Frosting

1¾ cups (425 ml) sugar
½ cup (125 ml) water
4 tablespoons corn syrup
2 egg whites, beaten
⅛ teaspoon salt
1 teaspoon vanilla

1. Put the sugar, water, and corn syrup on to cook in a heavy saucepan, heating slowly and stirring until all the sugar is dissolved.
2. Then cook rapidly without stirring until the syrup forms a firm ball in water (about 245°F/118°C on a candy thermometer).
3. Pour over the beaten egg whites slowly, beating meanwhile.
4. Add the flavoring, continue to beat until thick and ready to spread. This icing will keep in a covered jar in the refrigerator. Add a few drops of hot water to make of a consistency to spread.

Note: For detailed instructions about using a candy thermometer, see page 144.

Caramel Nut Frosting

2 cups (500 ml) sugar
1 cup (250 ml) thin sweet or sour cream
3 tablespoons caramel syrup
1 tablespoon butter
1 teaspoon grated orange rind
Nutmeats

1. Boil the sugar, cream, and caramel syrup (see recipe for Burnt Sugar Cake on page 151) in a heavy saucepan until the mixture forms a soft ball in cold water (236–240°F/113–115°C on a candy thermometer).
2. Remove from the heat and let cool.
3. Add the butter and grated rind, and beat until thick and creamy.
4. Spread on the cake. Decorate the top with whole nutmeats.

Easy Fudge Icing

2 tablespoons softened butter
1 whole egg or 2 yolks
Few grains of salt
1 square chocolate, melted
½ teaspoon vanilla
2 cups (500 ml) powdered sugar
Cream as necessary

1. Put the butter, eggs, salt, and chocolate in a bowl and beat with a rotary beater until creamy.
2. Add the vanilla, powdered sugar, and enough cream to spread easily. Put on with even strokes, leaving a slightly ridged appearance.

Variation

Easy Cocoa Icing: To make with cocoa, in place of the chocolate, add 3 tablespoons cocoa with the powdered sugar and increase the butter by 1 tablespoon.

Prune Filling

½ cup (125 ml) sugar
1 tablespoon flour
⅛ teaspoon salt
¼ teaspoon cinnamon
½ cup (125 ml) sour cream
1 cup (250 ml) prunes, puréed
1 egg, beaten
1 tablespoon lemon juice

1. Mix the dry ingredients in the top of a double boiler.
2. Add the cream, prunes, and egg.
3. Cook until thickened over hot water, about 20 minutes. Add the lemon juice and cool.

Cream Cheese Filling

8 ounces (227 g) cream cheese
½ cup (125 ml) drained chopped fruit (cherries, pineapple, apricots)
Cream to moisten

1. Blend the cream cheese and fruit with enough cream to make a smooth filling.
2. Spread between layers of warm gingerbread or spice cake, or use as a frosting.

Hard Sauce

⅓ cup (80 ml) butter
1 cup (250 ml) powdered sugar
½ teaspoon vanilla
Nutmeg

Cream the butter in a mixing bowl. Add the sugar gradually. Flavor.

Variations

Brown Sugar Sauce: Use brown sugar, first sifted to remove the lumps, and add to the butter instead of the powdered sugar. Then add ¼ cup (60 ml) thick cream and blend.
Cocoa Sauce: Blend in 2 tablespoons cocoa with the powdered sugar and add a few grains salt.

Custard Sauce

1 cup (250 ml) milk
2 egg yolks
2 tablespoons sugar
Few drops vanilla

1. Scald the milk in the top of a double boiler.
2. Beat the egg yolks with the sugar in a bowl.
3. Add the hot milk gradually and carefully to the egg mixture, mix thoroughly, and return to the top of the double boiler.
4. Cook over hot water, stirring constantly, for about 20 minutes or until the custard coats the spoon. Remove immediately, flavor, and cool.

Chocolate Sundae Sauce

2 squares chocolate
¼ cup (60 ml) hot water
¼ cup (60 ml) light corn syrup
1 cup (250 ml) sugar
⅛ teaspoon salt
⅛ teaspoon cinnamon
¾ cup (185 ml) thin cream or evaporated milk
½ teaspoon vanilla

1. Melt the chocolate over slow heat in a heavy saucepan or over warm water in a double boiler.
2. Add the water and stir until smooth.
3. Add the syrup, sugar, salt, and cinnamon and cook to the soft ball stage (236–240°F/113–115°C on a candy thermometer).
4. Remove, cool slightly. Add the cream and vanilla, stirring until smooth. Use hot or cold over ice cream.

Butterscotch Sauce

1½ cups (375 ml) brown sugar
¼ cup (60 ml) light corn syrup
½ cup (125 ml) hot water
½ cup (125 ml) thin cream or evaporated milk
2 tablespoons butter

1. Cook the sugar, syrup, and water in a heavy saucepan to the soft ball stage (236–240°F/113–115°C on a candy thermometer).
2. Remove from the heat and let cool slightly.
3. Add the cream and butter and blend. Use hot or cold over ice cream.

Tutti Frutti Sauce

⅓ cup (80 ml) honey
1 cup (250 ml) light-colored preserve, as peach or apricot
2 tablespoons chopped maraschino cherries

Heat together the honey and preserve, until warm through. Add the cherries and use as a topping for ice cream.

Chapter 10

Pastry and Pies

Pies which Mother used to make were popular because Mother was too busy to spend overlong in the mixing, and Mother was a generous person when it came to putting in the things that make pies good. And, of course, a practiced hand made her results usually sure.

Use good, sweet-smelling lard or other fat in the pie crust and mix it up lightly. Many cooks find that a canvas tacked over their board and a stockinet case for their rolling pin make it easier to get an even, flaky crust.

As for fillings, make them generous. A smaller section of a fat pie is usually more attractive than a larger section of a thin one. Use deep tins, but allow a little longer baking and setting time with thick fillings. Individual pies or tarts give a party touch, especially when filled with glazed fresh fruits and topped with cream. Lattice top crusts are good with fruit pies.

Pastry shells bake best in a hot oven. Single crust pies with a custard filling should be started in a fairly hot oven to bake the under crust, then baked more slowly until the custard is done. Raw fruit pies also need a hot oven at first and then more moderate heat to cook the fruit through.

An ideal fruit pie has a flaky crust, well browned on top, a filling that is well done, juicy but not runny. Cream or custard pie fillings should be of a consistency to hold their shape but not actually stiff, with a crisp under crust.

—*The Farmer's Wife*

Plain Pastry

Yield: 2 crusts

1½ cups (375 ml) flour
½ teaspoon salt
½ cup (125 ml) lard
3–4 tablespoons ice cold water

1. Put the flour in a mixing bowl, add the salt, and cut in the shortening with a dough blender, sharp-tined fork, or finger tips, until the pieces are the size of small peas.
2. Add a little water at a time, mixing with a fork lightly until the dough can be shaped into a ball.
3. Divide the dough and roll out 1 crust at a time. Avoid overhandling the dough either in mixing it or in rolling out the crust. Work quickly, especially in warm weather so that the fat doesn't melt.

Note: To bake single crusts, heat the oven to 475°F/ 245°C. Lay the crust in a pin tin quite loosely and prick well over the bottom or fit over the bottom of an inverted tin. Bake for 8–10 minutes.

Variations

Pastry Shells: Shape the pie crust over the outside of muffin tins. Prick and bake as for a single crust.
Rich Pastry: Increase the fat by 2–3 tablespoons.
Cheese Straws: Roll the rich pastry until thin. Spread with a thin layer of grated cheese. Fold, roll, spread with more cheese. Continue until 4 or 5 layers of cheese have been rolled into the pastry. Cut into strips 4–5 inches long and ½ inch wide. Bake at 475°F/245°C for 10–12 minutes or until light golden brown.

Hot Water Pastry

Yield: 2 crusts

½–⅔ cup (125–160 ml) lard or shortening
¼ cup (60 ml) boiling water
1½ cups (375 ml) flour
½ teaspoon salt
½ teaspoon baking powder

1. Warm a bowl, put in the lard, add the boiling water, and beat until creamy.
2. Sift in the dry ingredients and mix well. Chill. Roll out.

Note: This makes rather a mealy, rich crust but not flaky in texture. The inexperienced cook will find it easy to make. The dough must be chilled before it can be rolled.

Old-Fashioned Apple Pie

Yield: Pastry for 2 crusts

1 quart (1 l) sliced apples
1 cup (250 ml) sugar
1 tablespoon flour
½ teaspoon cinnamon
2 tablespoons butter, melted
½ tablespoon lemon juice

1. Heat the oven to 425°F/220°C.
2. Line a 10-inch (25-cm) pie tin with a pastry crust.
3. Fill with sliced apples.
4. Mix the sugar, flour, and cinnamon, and cover the apples with the mixture. Pour the butter and lemon juice over the top of the sugar. Cover with the top crust. Cut slits in the top crust to allow the steam to escape during baking.
5. Bake for 15 minutes, then reduce the temperature to 350°F/175°C and bake until the apples are done, about 45 minutes.

Variations
Southern Style: Use ½ cup (125 ml) molasses in place of ½ cup (125 ml) of the sugar, and add ¼ teaspoon nutmeg.
With Cheese: Grate cheese over the top crust of the baked pie. Place in a warm oven until the cheese melts.

Deep Dish Apple Pie

6 apples, thinly sliced
1 cup (250 ml) sugar
1 teaspoon cinnamon
2 tablespoons water
2 tablespoons butter
Cobbler batter or plain pastry
Cream or hard sauce

1. Heat the oven to 425°F/220°C.
2. Put the apples into a deep pan or baking dish. Sprinkle with the sugar, cinnamon, and water. Dot with the butter.
3. Bake for 15–25 minutes or until the apples begin to steam.
4. Remove from the oven and spread with a cobbler batter (see recipe for Fruit Cobbler on page 142) or with plain pastry. Bake a further 25–30 minutes or until juice bubbles through crust. Serve with the cream or hard sauce.

Graham Cracker Pie Crust

18 graham crackers
¼ cup (60 ml) sugar
½ cup (125 ml) soft butter (not melted)

1. Roll the crackers fine. Reserve a few crumbs for the topping.
2. Mix to a moist paste with the sugar and butter.
3. Pat the mixture in a pie tin, pressing down firmly on the bottom and sides.

Note: Fill this crust with a cream filling. Cover with a meringue and sprinkle with a few graham cracker crumbs. Bake 15–20 minutes in a 350°F/175°C oven.

Individual Cherry Pies

2 cups (500 ml) drained, unsweetened cherries
¾ cup (185 ml) cherry juice
¾ cup (185 ml) sugar
2½ tablespoons tapioca
Baked individual pie shells
Whipped cream

1. Using the top of a double boiler placed on the stove, heat the cherries, juice, and ½ cup of the sugar to boiling.
2. Skim out the cherries.
3. Place the top of the double boiler on the heat again and add the tapioca to the juice and boil for 5 minutes.
4. Then cook the juice and tapioca over hot water in the double boiler until clear (time depends upon the kind of tapioca used). Add the cherries and the remaining sugar.
5. Cool, then pour into the baked individual pie shells. Top with the whipped cream before serving.

Cranberry and Raisin Pie

Yield: Pastry for 2 crusts

3 cups (750 ml) cranberries
1 cup (250 ml) raisins
1½ cups (375 ml) sugar
2 tablespoons flour

1. Heat the oven to 400°F/205°C.
2. Line a pie tin with pastry.
3. Cut the cranberries in halves. Mix the cranberries with the raisins, sugar, and flour.
4. Pour into the unbaked pie shell, make a lattice top crust, and bake for 40–50 minutes or until the crust is brown.

Home Baking Pays in Satisfaction and Cash

by Miriam J. Williams, September 1935

A saving of $20.00 each year is what home baking means to the average family, to quote from an exhibit by a Minnesota 4-H Club, a club of girls, by the way, whose members each baked, on the average, 500 loaves of bread a year.

But who will say that a saving in money can compare with the satisfaction which comes with the making of bread? What a chain of homey memories are forged out of such simple tasks as beating up a bubbling sponge, the deft kneading of a "batch," turning an ear to the faint crackle of stretching blisters when loaves are being made out, a peep into the oven to see if the bread looks as good as it smells, and finally cutting golden crusted slices for the blue-and-white bread plate.

What do you wish for most when you start to crumble up a yeast cake? That the bread will be light? Remember, then, that the yeast plant must be given a chance to grow. Reduced to baking terms, this means that moisture and food must be provided and that the temperature of the sponge and dough must be kept just right.

The skillful young woman who has made hundreds of home-sized bakings of bread to test the flour of a famous milling company feels that the temperature of the starting mixture of flour and liquid, in which the yeast plant starts to grow, is most important. If it is a winter day and the air in the kitchen likely to be a little chilly, allowance is made by using warmer water. The combined temperature of liquid and room should be around 160°F/70°C, we are told. A dairy thermometer is very helpful for the beginning bread maker. It may be used to test temperature of liquids and to keep in the sponge and dough during rising. A temperature of 80°F/25°C for sponge and dough generally brings the best results. If changing temperature is one of your troubles, try keeping the sponge or dough in a closed cupboard with a bowl of warm water beside it.

Good ingredients are as important as active yeast. Choose dependable flour, reliable as to milling and baking qualifications.

Each good bread maker has her own particular method of mixing and baking bread, but each has found that these things are important:

* Do not let the dough rise too long for best flavor and texture. Get the yeast at an active stage (sponge, liquid yeast "ferment," or compressed yeast) before

mixing into dough. Then allow rather short risings. Bread is less likely to be coarse and dark if it is worked down two or three times when just double in bulk rather than allowing it to rise a long time without working down.

✷ Handle lightly, kneading with a quick, springy motion. Dough should feel live and tender. Allow it to rest on the board between the time of cutting into pieces or rolling out and shaping into loaves or rolls.

✷ Do not add flour after the first kneading. Avoid a too-stiff dough through the addition of too much flour, for this makes dry, crumbly bread.

✷ Start baking in a hot oven (about 400°F/205°C) for the first 15 minutes until the loaves are lightly browned, then finish baking at a more moderate temperature. If bread is started in a too-slow oven, it continues rising and makes a porous, dry loaf.

Rhubarb Meringue Pie

Yield: Pastry for 1 crust

2½ tablespoons flour
1¼ cups (300 ml) sugar
3 egg yolks, beaten
2½ cups (625 ml) cut rhubarb
Grated rind of ½ lemon
Meringue

1. Heat the oven to 450°F/230°C.
2. Line an 8-inch (20-cm) pie tin with pastry.
3. Mix together the flour and sugar in a bowl. Add the egg yolks and mix well.
4. Add the rhubarb and lemon rind, mix, and pour into the unbaked pastry shell.
5. Bake for 15 minutes. Reduce the temperature to 350°F/175°C and bake for 20–25 minutes or until tender.
6. Top with the meringue (see recipe below), but bake for only 10–15 minutes or until a light brown.

Meringue

2 egg whites
Pinch salt
2–3 drops vanilla
4 tablespoons sugar

1. Heat the oven to 325°F/160°C.
2. Beat the egg whites in a mixing bowl until frothy.
3. Add the salt, vanilla, and sugar. Beat until it peaks.
4. Spread over the pie. Bake 15–20 minutes or until light brown. Let cool in a fairly warm place. A meringuue will not fall if baked and cooled slowly.

Pumpkin Pie

*Yield: Pastry for 1
generous crust*

2¼ cups (550 ml) cooked, strained pumpkin
1 cup (250 ml) brown sugar
1½ teaspoons cinnamon
⅛ teaspoon cloves, if desired
½ teaspoon nutmeg
½ teaspoon ginger
¾ teaspoon salt
3 eggs
1½ cups (375 ml) evaporated milk, scalded

1. Heat the oven to 400°F/205°C.
2. Line a deep 9-inch (22½-cm) pie tin with pastry. Shape a good rim. For a smaller tin, use two-thirds of the recipe.
3. Mix the pumpkin and sugar in a large bowl. Add the spices and salt.
4. Add the slightly beaten eggs and scalded milk. Mix well.
5. Pour into the unbaked pie shell and bake for 10 minutes to set the crust, reduce the temperature to 350°F/175°C, and bake for another 45 minutes or until a knife inserted in the center comes out clean.

Angel Cream Pie

½ cup (125 ml) sugar
2 tablespoons flour
⅛ teaspoon salt
1 pint (500 ml) thin cream, warmed slightly
1 teaspoon vanilla
2 egg whites, beaten stiff

1. Heat the oven to 400°F/205°C.
2. Line a 9-inch (22½-cm) pie tin with pastry.
3. Mix the dry ingredients and gradually stir in the cream.
4. Add the vanilla, and last, the stiff egg whites. Mix in lightly but thoroughly.
5. Pour into the unbaked crust and bake for 10 minutes. Reduce the heat to 350°F/175°C and bake for 35–40 minutes or until well set and lightly browned on top. Cool before serving.

Sour Cream Pie

Yield: Pastry for 1 crust

1 cup (250 ml) brown sugar
1 tablespoon flour
1½ teaspoons mixed spices
1 cup (250 ml) raisins
1 cup (250 ml) sour cream
2 egg yolks, beaten
1 tablespoon melted butter
1 teaspoon vanilla
Meringue

1. Heat the oven to 400°F/205°C.
2. Line a 9-inch (22½-cm) pie tin with pastry.
3. Mix the sugar, flour, spices (see recipe for Fluffy Spice Cake on page 151), and raisins.
4. To the sour cream, add the egg yolks, butter, and vanilla.
5. Add the raisin mixture to the cream mixture.
6. Pour into the unbaked pie shell. Bake for 10 minutes, then reduce the heat to 350°F/175°C, and bake for 35–40 minutes or until well set. Top with the meringue (see recipe page 186).

Custard Pie

Yield: Pastry for 1 crust

2½ cups (625 ml) milk
3 eggs
½ cup (125 ml) sugar
¼ teaspoon salt
1 teaspoon vanilla
Nutmeg, grated

1. Heat the oven to 425°F/220°C.
2. Line an 8-inch (20-cm) pie tin with pastry. Make a good rim on the crust to keep the filling in. The crust may be chilled while making the custard.
3. Scald the milk and add to the eggs, slightly beaten, with the sugar, salt, and vanilla.
4. Strain the mixture into the unbaked pie crust and grate the nutmeg over the top of the custard.
5. Bake for 15 minutes, to set the crust. Reduce the heat to 325°F/160°C and bake for 20 minutes or until the custard is firm and a knife dipped in hot water and inserted in the center of the custard comes out clean.

Variation

Coconut Custard: Substitute 1 cup (250 ml) cream for 1 cup (250 ml) of the milk. Omit the nutmeg, and add ½ cup (125 ml) moist canned coconut before baking.

Mincemeat For Pies

4 pounds (2 kg) lean beef
Beef stock
10 pounds (9½ kg) tart apples, chopped
2 pounds (1 kg) beef suet, chopped
3 pounds (1½ kg) sugar
3 pounds (1½ kg) currants
3 pounds (1½ kg) seeded raisins
½ pound (250 g) citron, cut fine
2 oranges, rind and juice
2 cups (500 ml) molasses
1½ quarts cider
1 quart pickled peach juice
1 glass currant jelly
1 tablespoon cinnamon
1 tablespoon nutmeg
1 teaspoon allspice
Salt to season

1. Simmer the meat until tender in sufficient beef stock to cover. Drain and preserve the stock. Reduce the stock to 1 cup (250 ml). Cool and chop the meat.
2. Combine all the ingredients in a large kettle. Heat gradually and simmer until the apples are cooked.
3. Seal in glass jars and refrigerate until ready for use.

Note: For pies, bake the mincemeat between 2 pastry crusts at 400°F/205°C for 30–35 minutes.

Meal Planning When Children Are in School

by Miriam J. Williams, October 1935

Eight or nine months of the year, five days a week, mothers of rural school children are waving them out the door, with a silent wish for good health, good behavior, good report cards. Breakfast and lunch boxes are already off the list, but there are still a hundred and one things to crowd into the morning.

But if it's first things first, what in the way of household tasks can rank higher in importance than giving time for thought as to what goes into those lunch boxes and into the other two meals when all are at home?

Food is our faithful servant only if we select it wisely. It takes planning to make it work for strong bones and well bodies.

A time for meal planning on one day each week is a truly good habit. I know one capable homemaker who allows Monday for picking up after Sunday, collecting and sorting clothes, and for planning meals and work for the week. She claims that it "eases" her into Tuesday's washday with a feeling that things are all set and ready to go, a feeling which usually lasts all week. On Monday, she makes a trip to the cellar to bring up vegetables and canned stuff for several meals, and to remind herself of the way this supply may best be distributed through the week.

Her meals are actually written down in black and white, although they are flexible enough to allow for changes. Family favorites are not forgotten, nor are the same dishes repeated to the saturation point. The needs of the two youngsters at home, of the two in school, and the hard-working father are all considered. These menus are later filed, valuable for reference in planning for canning and for quantity buying.

I can't help but feel sorry for those children who have a hurried breakfast of cereal and toast, a lunch of sandwiches, sweets, and occasionally fruit, and then come home to a supper of warmed-over meat and indifferent vegetables. What are they getting? An overabundance of starches and sweets, a fair amount of protein, a very limited amount of regulating and protective food. Where meals are habitually low in vegetables, fruit, and milk, children are headed for dietary and dental troubles.

Chapter 11

Jellies, Conserves, and Jams

Spreads that are made with fruit include: preserves, jams, jellies, conserves, marmalades, and fruit butters. A definition of these different forms may help in understanding recipes and in exhibiting at the fair.

❧ Jelly: A transparent quivery mixture of fruit juice and sugar (sometimes with added pectin and acid), which, when unmolded, holds its shape. Tender, not syrupy or tough.

❧ Preserve: Whole fruit, or distinct pieces of fruit, transparent. Tender, crisp in a heavy syrup.

❧ Jam: Small fruits and sugar cooked to a "spreading" consistency, usually not in distinct or whole pieces.

❧ Marmalade: Similar to preserve, but usually with some citrus fruit.

❧ Conserve: Similar to marmalade with the addition of nuts or raisins.

❧ Butter: Smooth, quite thick, but of spreading consistency; usually made from sieved fruit pulp, spice, and sugar. The pulp left after the extraction of the juice is sometimes used this way.

—*The Farmer's Wife*

Jellies

Jelly Making

Proper preparation and storage of home-canned food products are essential. At the end of this section are details of the USDA recommended equipment and containers, recommended methods for their sterilization, as well as information regarding sealing containers and storage of jellied fruits. Read this information carefully.

* Importance of Pectin: Fruit juice and sugar will not always make jelly of the description given. The fruit must have a certain amount of pectin and acid or else they must be supplied. A combination of fruit low in pectin with one rich in pectin will often bring about a good texture. Commercial pectin can be purchased in liquid or powdered form. Carefully follow directions that come with these products.

Fruit juices rich in natural pectin and acid that may be used alone in jelly making, if not overripe, include: currant, grape, sour apple, crab apple, plum, raspberry, blackberry, cranberry, gooseberry, and quince.

Fruit juices that require the addition of commercial pectin or a combination with one of the above are: cherry, strawberry, rhubarb, sweet apple, peach, pear, pineapple, and some others.

* Extracting Juice: Use sound, not overripe fruit. Wash and cut in pieces, if large. Add only a very little water to juicy fruits, such as grapes and berries. Add water to cover apples and hard fruits. Cover and cook slowly only until soft. Mash and strain though a jelly bag or several thicknesses of cheesecloth, first scalded. Do not squeeze or a cloudy jelly will result. Juice may be canned and then made into jelly during the winter.

* Second Extraction for Fruits Rich in Pectin, as Grapes, Sour Apples: Use pulp from the first extraction, cover with water and stir. Cook slowly, strain as before. Combine two extractions or boil the second extraction down about a third before measuring for sugar if it is used alone.

* Proportion of Sugar: The general rule is ¾ cup (185 ml) sugar to each cup of juice. Equal parts sugar and juice usually make a sweet, too-soft jelly; too little sugar makes a tough jelly. However, juice rich in pectin, as currant, grape, and some berry juice, may require equal parts sugar and juice. Make a pectin test and if there is a decided precipitate, use the larger amount of sugar.

* Pectin Test: Add 1 teaspoon cooked, cooled fruit juice to 1 tablespoon denatured alcohol. Stir slightly to mix. Juices rich in pectin will form a solid jellylike mass. Juices low in pectin will form small particles of jellylike material.

Caution: Denatured alcohol is poisonous. Do not taste the tested juice. Wash all utensils used in this test thoroughly.

❧Jelly Tests: When the syrup "sheets off" the spoon or two drops run together as one from the side of the spoon, the jelly is done. With a jelly or candy thermometer, cook the syrup until it registers between 214–218°F/101–103°C.

How To Make Jelly

Note: Make only 1½–2 quarts of juice into jelly at a time.
1. Measure the sugar according to the rule above and let it warm through.
2. Boil the juice rapidly for 5 minutes, removing the scum.
3. Add the sugar slowly, stirring until all is dissolved. Boil the juice rapidly until the jelly test is secured.
4. Remove from the stove, let stand a few minutes, and skim.
5. Pour the hot juice in hot, sterilized glasses. Cover with a thin layer of paraffin while hot.

Combinations of Fruit Juices Which Are Pleasing: ·

Extract the juice as directed, combine in equal parts as a rule, and measure for the sugar. Follow directions above.
❧ Apple And Strawberry, with a little lemon juice for flavor
❧ Apple And Cherry
❧ Apple or Currant And Blackberry, With Raspberry or Elderberry
❧ Apple And Plum
❧ Currant or Apple And Rhubarb
❧ Apple And Quince
❧ Apple Flavored With Mint: Pour boiling water over the mint leaves, equal parts. Let stand 1 hour. Use 2 tablespoons of this mint extraction to each cup apple juice.
❧ Apple Flavored With Rose Geranium: Wash the geranium leaves and put one in each jelly glass.

Venison Jelly

Note: This spiced jelly is particularly good with wild game, and it makes a pleasant change from ordinary grape jelly.

1. When making grape jelly, tie a small piece of cinnamon and 2 dozen cloves in a cheesecloth.
2. Drop this into the boiling juice and remove before pouring the jelly.

June Jelly

1 pint (500 ml) cherries, stoned
2 quarts (2 l) currants
1 quart (1 l) strawberries
1 quart (1 l) raspberries
2 cups (500 ml) apple juice
Sugar

1. Cook the fruits together until soft. Strain through a jelly bag.
2. Add the apple juice and test for pectin, to find how much sugar is needed, usually ¾ cup (185 ml) per cup of juice.
3. Add the sugar and cook until it responds to a jelly test.
4. Pour in jelly glasses or molds.

Cranberry Jelly

1 quart (1 l) berries
2 cups (500 ml) water
2 cups (500 ml) sugar

1. Cook the cranberries until soft. Press through a sieve.
2. Add the sugar and stir until dissolved.
3. Boil for about 5 minutes or until it responds to a jelly test.
4. Pour in glasses or molds.

Variation

Spiced Cranberry Jelly: Tie in a bag 1 tablespoon whole cloves, 2 or 3 allspice berries, a cinnamon stick. Boil with the cranberries, then remove.

Summer Spreads

Rhubarb Conserve

4 pounds (2 kg) rhubarb
5 pounds (2¼ kg) sugar
1 pound (½ kg) seeded raisins
Rind and juice of 2 oranges
Juice of 1 lemon

1. Cut the rhubarb in 1-inch (2½-cm) pieces and put in a preserving kettle.
2. Add the sugar, raisins, grated orange rind, and juice of the oranges and lemon. Mix, cover, and let stand for 30 minutes.
3. Place on the stove, bring to the boiling point and let simmer for 45 minutes, stirring frequently.
4. Pour in hot, sterile glasses or jars and seal.
5. Process for 5 minutes in a boiling water bath.

Variation

With Nuts: Add ½ pound (250 g) chopped nuts.

Strawberry Preserves

4 cups (1000 ml) strawberries
5 cups (1250 ml) sugar
½ cup (125 ml) lemon juice

1. Wash and hull the berries. Cover with the sugar and let stand overnight.
2. In the morning, bring to a boil in a kettle. Boil for exactly 7 minutes.
3. Add the lemon juice. Boil for 3 minutes.
4. Remove from the fire, stirring occasionally until nearly cold. This will keep the berries suspended in the syrup.
5. Pour in sterilized glasses and seal.
6. Process for 5 minutes in a boiling water bath.

Sun Cherry Preserves

2 pints (1000 ml) pitted cherries
2 pints (1000 ml) sugar

1. Wash and pit the cherries and rinse well.
2. Put the cherries in a kettle and add the sugar. Heat slowly at first and then bring to a boil. Boil rapidly for 12 minutes.
3. Pour into shallow dishes and set in the sun under glass for protection until the juice is thick.
4. Reheat, pack in jars, and seal.
5. Process for 5 minutes in a boiling water bath.

Peach Jam

9 peaches
1 orange
Sugar

1. Remove the skin and stones from the peaches. Put through a coarse food chopper.
2. Wash the orange, cut, and put it through the food chopper.
3. Measure the fruit pulp and take an equal measure of the sugar.
4. Cook in a kettle until it responds to a jelly test.
5. Pack in jars and seal.
6. Process for 5 minutes in a boiling water bath.

Concord Grape Marmalade

1. Wash the concord grapes, drain, and remove the stems. Separate the pulp from the skins.
2. Cook the pulp slowly in a kettle until the seeds separate. Rub through a fine strainer.
3. Add the skins to the pulp, measure, and add three-quarters of the pulp and skins in sugar.
4. Cook slowly for 30 minutes.
5. Pack in jars and seal.
6. Process for 5 minutes in a boiling water bath.

Variation

Conserve: Add the grated rind and juice of an orange to the concord grape pulp and skin and sugar before cooking as in the Grape Marmalade recipe. Five minutes before removing from the heat, add the nuts. Proportions: 4 pints (2000 ml) grapes, 1 pint (500 ml) orange, 1 cup (250 ml) nuts. Pack in jars and seal. Process for 5 minutes in a boiling water bath.

Apple and Tomato Butter

6 cups (1500 ml) apple pulp
6 cups (1500 ml) cooked, strained tomatoes
5 cups (1250 ml) sugar
4 sticks cinnamon
2 tablespoons whole cloves
½ cup (125 ml) vinegar

1. Press the apple pulp through a coarse strainer into a kettle. (The apple pulp left after the juice has drained off for apple jelly may be used.)
2. Add the tomatoes and sugar.
3. Tie the spices in a cheesecloth and boil for 30 minutes with the other ingredients.
4. Add the vinegar, boil for 10 minutes, remove the spices, put into hot, clean glasses, and seal.
5. Process for 5 minutes in a boiling water bath.

Winter Spreads

These can be made in the less busy seasons or when the summer supply is gone.

Amber Marmalade

1 grapefruit
1 orange
1 lemon
3½ quarts (3½ l) water
Sugar

1. Wash the fruit and cut in paper-thin slices, using a very sharp knife. Add the water and let stand overnight.
2. Cook in a preserving kettle until the peel is tender. Again let the mixture stand overnight.
3. Measure the fruit and add an equal amount of sugar, and cook until the syrup thickens when dropped on a cold dish.
3. Pack and seal in clean, hot jars.
4. Process for 5 minutes in a boiling water bath.

Carrot, Apple and Peach Conserve

2 cups (500 ml) shredded or grated carrots
2 cups (500 ml) diced tart apples
3 cups (750 ml) sugar
1 cup (250 ml) peaches, canned or stewed, and
    cut fine
Juice of 1 lemon

1. Mix all the ingredients in a kettle and simmer until the mixture is clear, stirring to prevent burning.
2. Pack into clean, hot jars and seal.
3. Process for 5 minutes in a boiling water bath.

Cranberry Conserve

1 quart (1 l) cranberries
2 oranges
2 cups (500 ml) cold water
1 cup (250 ml) raisins, chopped
4 cups (1000 ml) sugar
2 cups (500 ml) boiling water
1 cup (250 ml) nutmeats

1. Run the cranberries and oranges through a food chopper.
2. Put the fruit in a kettle, add the cold water, and cook until the cranberries are soft.
3. Add the raisins, sugar, and boiling water. Cook until thick. Add the nuts, and remove from the fire.
4. Pour into clean, hot jelly glasses and cover.
5. Process for 5 minutes in a boiling water bath.

USDA Recommendations for Processing and Storing Jellied Fruit Products

Rotary Food Press

Equipment

✶ A large kettle is essential. To bring mixture to a full boil without boiling over, use an 8- or 10-quart (8- or 10-l) kettle with a broad flat bottom.

✶ A jelly bag or a fruit press may be used for extracting fruit juice for jellies. The bag may be made of several thicknesses of closely woven cheesecloth, of firm unbleached muslin, or canton flannel with napped side in. Use a jelly bag or cheesecloth to strain pressed juice. A special stand or colander will hold the jelly bag.

✶ A jelly, candy, or deep-fat thermometer is an aid in making fruit products without added pectin.

✶ Other equipment that may be useful includes a quart measure, measuring cups and spoons, paring and utility knives, food chopper, masher, reamer, grater, bowls, wire basket, colander, long-handled spoon, ladle, clock with second hand, and household scale.

Containers

❧ Jelly glasses or canning jars may be used as containers for jellied fruit products. Be sure all jars and closures are perfect. Discard any with cracks or chips; defects prevent airtight seals.

❧ For jellies to be sealed with paraffin, use glasses or straight-sided containers that will make an attractive mold.

❧ For jams, preserves, conserves, and marmalades, use canning jars with lids that can be tightly sealed and processed. Paraffin tends to loosen and break the seal on these products.

❧ Get glasses or jars ready before you start to make the jellied product. Wash containers in warm, soapy water and rinse with hot water. Sterilize jelly containers in boiling water for 10 minutes (beyond point that water resumes boiling). Keep all containers hot, either in a slow oven or in hot water, until they are used. This will prevent containers from breaking when filled with hot jelly or jam.

❧ Wash and rinse all lids and bands. Metal lids with sealing compound may need boiling or holding in boiling water for a few minutes. Follow the manufacturer's directions. Use new lids; bands and jars may be reused.

❧ If you use porcelain-lined zinc caps, have clean, new rings of the right size for jars. Wash rings in hot, soapy water. Rinse well.

Filling and Sealing Containers

Prepare canning jars and lids or jelly glasses as directed above.

❧ To Seal with Lids: Fill hot jars to ⅛ inch (¼ cm) of top with hot jelly or fruit mixture. Wipe jar rim clean, place hot metal lid on jar with sealing compound next to glass. Screw metal band down firmly, and stand jar upright to cool.

❧ Work quickly when packing and sealing jars. To keep fruit from floating to the top, gently shake jars of jam occasionally as they cool.

❧ To Seal with Paraffin: Use this method only with jelly. Pour hot jelly mixture immediately into hot containers to within ½ inch (1 cm) of top. Cover with hot paraffin. Use only enough paraffin to make a layer ⅛ inch (¼ cm) thick. A single thin layer, that can expand or contract readily, gives a better seal than one thick layer or two thin layers. Prick air bubbles in paraffin. Bubbles cause holes as paraffin hardens, and may prevent a good seal. Use a double boiler for melting paraffin and keeping it hot without reaching smoking temperature.

❧ To Process Jams, Conserves, Marmalades, and Preserves: Inexpensive enamelware canners may be purchased at most hardware or variety stores. However, any large metal container may be used, if it:

❧ Is deep enough to allow for 1 or 2 inches of water above the tops of the jars, plus a little extra space for boiling (2–4 inches or 5–10 cm space above jars is ideal).

❋ Has a close fitting cover.

❋ Has a wire or wood rack with partitions to keep jars from touching each other or the bottom or sides of the container.

Put filled home-canning jars into a water bath canner or a container filled with hot water. Add hot water, if needed, to bring water an inch or two over tops of jars. Bring water to a rolling boil gently for 5 minutes.

Remove jars from canner after processing. Cool away from drafts before storing.

Storing Jellied Fruit Products

❋ Let products stand undisturbed overnight to avoid breaking gel. Cover jelly glasses with metal or paper lids. Label with name, date, and lot number, if you make more than one lot a day. Store in cool, dry place; the shorter the storage time, the better the eating quality of the product.

❋ Uncooked jams may be held up to 3 weeks in a refrigerator. For longer storage, they should be placed in a freezer.

Canning *for the* Fair

by Doris W. McCray, July 1928

The premiums for canned goods at the county fair may not be large, but several of them added together make dollars worth winning. Besides, there is the fun and honor of capturing a few ribbons.

Canning for exhibit is not difficult. In the years that I have been judging and exhibiting, I have observed that the women who win are ambitious, but generally have had no special training. With help from the home demonstration agent or from some state bulletin, they experimented until their results were good. If there is little competition, they win even though their jars score only 90 percent.

Fruit

When doing your usual canning, separate the fruit which is most perfect for exhibit. This fruit should be uniform in size, fully ripened, yet quite firm, and of the very finest flavor and color.

The open kettle, cold pack, or hot pack method may be used; however the cold pack is easiest, since the pieces of fruit may be readily arranged in the jars.

When put into jars hot, it is more difficult to arrange the fruit nicely.

Some premium lists specify pints or quarts and disqualify the other size. By writing to the fair secretary you may obtain a premium list. Usually fruit, vegetables, meat, and pickles are in quarts; preserves and jams in pints; and jelly in half-pints.

Pack fairly closely, fill with boiling syrup, and process. Shrinkage during processing will make the total volume of the fruit about two-thirds the contents of the jar, and the liquid one-third. Overcooking may make the edges of the fruit ragged, or the syrup cloudy.

The color of the canned fruit should be that of perfect, fresh fruit, not faded or darkened from too long cooking. A thin syrup is desirable for exhibiting. A thick honeylike syrup places the fruit in the class of preserves. To prevent peaches and apples from darkening when peeled, pack in jars and cover at once with hot syrup, or if they must stand before packing, cover with syrup or water with lemon juice in it. Fruit must appear free from all blemishes, carefully prepared, in perfect condition.

The label looks best when typed or printed, stating the kind of fruit, method of canning, and date canned. The name of the exhibitor must not appear. The label is placed squarely upon the jar a little above the center.

Strawberries will float on top of the liquid unless cooked and then allowed to stand overnight to absorb the syrup and become plump. They are quite acid and require very little cooking. The less cooking, the better will be their color and shape.

Vegetables

Vegetables are judged by the same card as that used for fruits, except that clearness and brightness of color of the vegetable are considered rather than clearness and density of syrup. The liquid should have no sediment, and there should be just enough to fill the spaces between the vegetables and insure that they are not packed too tight for perfect processing.

Tomatoes for exhibit are covered with water or strained tomato juice. For sale, only crushed tomatoes are allowed. Beets shrink less than you expect and if the jars are too full, they press tightly against the glass, making gray spots. Pack your beets loosely.

Vegetables should appear neat and perfect. Ends of string beans are cut off with scissors, or a knife on a breadboard, diagonally or straight. Every imperfection must be carefully removed. The edges of carrots will appear ragged if they are cooked too long before peeling and packing.

Grade carefully, selecting the young, tender products for exhibit. If peas are not graded, the young ones will split open, making the liquid cloudy before the old ones are cooked. String beans should not be tough and stringy; peas should be tender, not mealy; spinach tender and green, not woody; beets not coarse grained nor fibrous. While the jars are not opened, it is easy to judge the eating quality of vegetables.

Pickles on Display

For pickles, a bright green color is best, though alum should not be used in obtaining it. Pickles should be uniform in size, either small, medium, or large. They should be well-shaped, plump, not shrunken. They are packed as closely as possible, yet not squeezed or crushed, so that the jar is comfortably full.

Sweet pickles are more difficult to make, yet if you start out with sour pickles, adding sugar gradually from one day to the next, they will not shrivel. Placing in a too-sweet syrup at once causes shrivelling.

Relishes should be pretty colors, a variety of vegetables which taste well together, cut into uniformly fine pieces, with clear liquid.

Meats

If canning meats for exhibit, the pieces should be neatly cut, without ragged edges, as large as will go into wide-mouthed jars. A rich, dark brown color is desirable, the result of roasting the meat. It is seared in a hot oven, then finished in a slow oven before cutting, packing in jars, and processing.

The meat may be precooked by boiling, but the color and flavor will not be so fine. Sausage cakes are fried enough to about half-cook them. Chicken may be fried, without flouring it, just long enough to make an attractive brown. Precooking is necessary to shrink meat. If it is merely blanched, a reddish scum

will form in the can during processing, which is unattractive.

A little caramelized sugar can be added to the pan gravy, which is strained through cheesecloth into the jars after packing them with meat. No extra water is added, since the jars need not be full. The gravy should be so rich that the gelatin hardens.

There should be two-thirds meat, and one-third liquid, after canning, with only enough fat to keep the meat juicy. If the meat is very fat, it should be trimmed off before canning, to avoid a greasy flavor.

The meat must be young, tender, firm, and fine grained, never overcooked.

It should not be scorched, but nicely browned. The skin of chicken requires thorough scrubbing and cutting with shears to remove imperfections. Meat should look unusually good to eat.

Preserves

A perfect preserve consists of firm, fine-textured, whole, plump, colorful, good-flavored fruit, in a rich honeylike, clear syrup.

The fruit and syrup are two distinct parts. The fruit should not be shrivelled, mashed, or broken into irregular pieces. The thick, transparent syrup can readily be distinguished from the thinner syrup of canned fruit and the jellied fruit juice of marmalade.

Ideal Jelly

The container should be neat, not sticky. Duplex-seal jelly glasses in half-pint size are best, since a quarter-turn of the wrist opens them, and they can be tightly covered after judging. A thin layer of paraffin is removed by the judge, and replaced, since the jelly will not be spoiled by opening. The label is neatly pasted a little above the center of the glass.

Ideal jelly cuts easily because it is so tender, yet the angles made by cutting are retained. It must never be tough, but should display a quivering expectancy, so that it barely holds its shape if turned from the mold.

Jellies will be crystal clear if the jelly bag is not squeezed, and if the juice is then allowed to drip through flannel or felt. The color should be bright and sparkling, not too dark from long, slow cooking, nor too pale from selecting the wrong variety of fruit or adding too much water to extract juice.

Good jelly should never be syrupy, tough, gummy, brittle, scorched, or insipid, nor should it contain crystals. Do not exhibit grape jelly which has been made for some time. Make it fresh. If made without using the grape skins in extracting juice, it will not form crystals, but it lacks color.

Chapter 12

Pickles
and Relishes

Pickled fruits, relishes, and variations of cucumber pickles, to be served with meat courses, have risen to new popularity in the last few years. Pickled foods add just the tang to the main course that is needed. If you have not been including pickled fruits in your canning budget, we suggest that you try a few jars this year. You'll enjoy them!

—*The Farmer's Wife*

Pickles

Just as with jellies, proper preparation and storage of home-canned pickles is essential. At the end of this section are details of USDA recommended equipment and containers, recommended methods for their sterilization, as well as information regarding sealing containers and storage of pickles—all to insure acceptable quality and bacteriological safety of the pickled product. Read this information carefully.

Common Causes of Poor Quality Pickles

❧ Shriveled Pickles: Shriveling may result from using too strong a vinegar, sugar, or salt solution at the start of the pickling process. In making the very sweet or very sour pickles, it is best to start with a dilute solution and increase gradually to the desired strength. Overcooking or overprocessing may also cause shriveling.

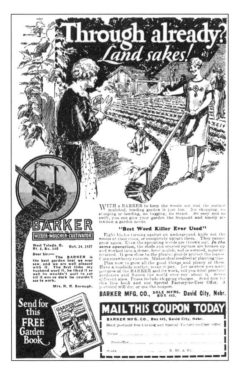

❧ Hollow Pickles: Hollowness usually results from either poorly developed cucumbers, keeping cucumbers too long before pickling, too rapid fermentation, or too strong or too weak a brine.

❧ Soft or Slippery Pickles: These generally result from microbial action that causes spoilage. Microbial activity may be caused by too little salt or acid, cucumbers not covered with brine during fermentation, scum scattered throughout the brine during the fermentation period, insufficient heat treatment, a seal that is not airtight, moldy garlic or spices. Blossoms, if not entirely removed from the cucumbers, may contain certain fungi or yeasts responsible for enzymatic softening of pickles.

❧ Dark Pickles: Darkness my be caused by use of ground spices, too much spice, iodized salt, overcooking, minerals in water (especially iron), and use of iron utensils.

Texture Tricks in Pickles

by Miriam J. Williams, September 1935

When is a pickle a good pickle? Let an experienced judge of food products give the answer: "A pickle must have snap," she says. "It should add interest to a meal which already has enough bland, mild-flavored food. It must not be disagreeably sharp, for most people prefer a very slightly sweet taste along with the acid. Is there anything more sad then a soft, slippery pickle?"

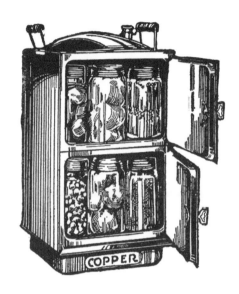

Sometimes, the judge said, the vegetables are cooked too long, as in mustard pickles or spiced fruit pickles. More often, the failure to get crispness is due to insufficient curing, or perhaps poor vinegar.

Remember that pickles need time. Almost all kinds need to stand in the jars to develop flavor before they are opened for use, unless they are cured by the long process. Whole cucumber pickles take more time than chunk, and chunk pickles more time than sliced. The success of cucumber pickles depends upon curing (the salt water changed for the fresh water in the vegetables) and then development of flavor.

Brined Dill Pickles

Yield: 9–10 quarts (8½–9½ l)

Pickles and First Brine Ingredients

20 pounds (about ½ bushel or 9 kg) cucumbers, 3–6 inches (7½–15 cm) long
¾ cup (185 ml) whole mixed pickling spice
2–3 bunches of dill plant, fresh or dried
2½ cups (625 ml) vinegar
1¾ cups (425 ml) pure, granulated salt
2½ gallons (9½ l) water

Last Brine Ingredients

½ cup (125 ml) salt
4 cups (1000 ml) vinegar
1 gallon (3¾ l) water
Dill
1–2 cloves garlic per 1 quart (1 l) jar

Sing A Song of Canning Time
August 1912

Sing a song of
canning-time,
Sweetness everywhere;
Sugar, spice, and all
things nice
Scenting all the air,
Pickles, butter, jelly, jam,
Load the cellar shelves;
Aren't we proud to
know that we
Made 'em all ourselves.

1. Cover the cucumbers with cold water. Wash thoroughly, using a vegetable brush; handle gently to avoid bruising. Take care to remove any blossoms. Drain or wipe dry.

2. Place half the spices and a layer of dill in a 5-gallon (19-l) crock or jar. Fill with the cucumbers to within 3 or 4 inches (7½–10 cm) of the top. Place a layer of the dill and the remaining spices over the top. Thoroughly mix the vinegar, salt, and water and pour over the cucumbers.

3. Cover with a heavy china or glass plate or lid that fits inside the crock. Use a weight to hold the plate down and keep the cucumbers under the brine. A glass jar or plastic bag filled with water makes a good weight (see details on page 214). Cover crock loosely with a clean cloth.

4. Keep the pickles at room temperature and remove any scum daily when formed. Scum may start forming in 3–5 days. Do not stir the pickles, but be sure they are completely covered with the brine. If necessary, make additional brine, using the original proportions.

5. In about 3 weeks, the cucumbers will have become an olive-green color and should have the desirable flavor. Any white spots inside the cucumbers will disappear in processing.

6. Make a last, fresh brine, using ½ cup (125 ml) salt and 4 cups (1000 ml) vinegar to 1 gallon (3¾ l) of water. Strain before it is heated to boiling.

7. Pack the pickles, along with some of the dill, into clean, hot quart jars; add 1 or 2 garlic cloves per jar. Avoid too tight a pack. Cover with the boiling brine to ½ inch from the top of the jar. Adjust the jar lids.

8. Process in boiling water for 15 minutes (adjust for altitude, according to the directions on page 216). Start to count the processing time as soon as the hot jars are placed in the actively boiling water.

9. Remove the jars and complete the seals, if necessary. Set the jars upright on a wire rack or folded towel to cool. Place them several inches apart.

Fresh-Pack Dill Pickles

Yield: 7 quarts (6½ l)

17–18 pounds (7½–8 kg) cucumbers, 3–5 inches (7½–12½ cm) long

5 percent brine water made of ¾ cup (185 ml) pure, granulated salt per 1 gallon (3¾ l) water

2 gallons (7½ l) vinegar

¾ cup (185 ml) pure, granulated salt

¼ cup (60 ml) sugar

2¼ quarts (2 l) water

2 tablespoons whole mixed pickling spices

2 teaspoons whole mustard seed per quart jar

1–2 cloves garlic per quart jar

3 heads of dill plant, fresh or dried, per quart jar, or

1 tablespoon dill seed per quart jar

1. Wash the cucumbers thoroughly. Scrub with a vegetable brush and drain.

2. Cover with 5 percent brine. Let set overnight. Drain.

3. Combine the vinegar, salt, sugar, and water, and the pickling spices that are tied in a clean, thin, white cloth. Heat the mixture to boiling.

4. Pack the cucumbers into clean, hot jars. Add the mustard seed, dill plant or seed, and garlic to each jar. Cover with the boiling liquid to within ½ inch (1 cm) from top of the jar. Adjust the jar lids.

5. Process in boiling water for 20 minutes, starting to count as soon as the hot jars are placed in the actively boiling water.

6. Remove the jars and compete the seals, if necessary. Set the jars upright on a wire rack or folded towel to cool. Place them several inches apart.

Crosscut Pickle Slices

Yield: 3½ quarts (3¼ l)

4 quarts (about 6 pounds or 2¾ kg) cucumbers, medium size, sliced
1½ cups (375 ml) white onions, small, sliced
2 large garlic cloves
⅓ cup (80 ml) salt
2 quarts (2 l) ice, crushed or cubes
4–4½ cups (1000–1125 ml) sugar (less sugar results in a less sweet pickle)
1½ teaspoons turmeric
1½ teaspoons celery seed
2 tablespoons mustard seed
3 cups (750 ml) white vinegar

1. Wash the cucumbers thoroughly. Scrub with a vegetable brush and drain.
2. Slice the unpeeled cucumbers into ⅛- to ½-inch (¼- to 1-cm) slices; discard the ends. Add the onions and garlic. Add the salt and mix thoroughly. Cover with the ice and let stand for 3 hours. Drain thoroughly. Remove the garlic.
3. Combine the sugar, spices, and vinegar. Heat the mixture to boiling. Add the drained cucumbers and onions. Heat for 5 minutes.
4. Pack the hot pickles loosely into clean, hot pint jars and cover with the hot liquid to ½ inch from the top. Adjust the jar lids.
5. Process in boiling water for 5 minutes (adjust for altitude according to the directions on page 216), starting to count as soon as the hot jars are placed in the actively boiling water.
6. Remove the jars and compete the seals, if necessary. Set the jars upright on a wire rack or folded towel to cool. Place them several inches apart.

Sweet Gherkins

Yield: 3–3½ quarts (2¾–3¼ l)

5 quarts (4¾ l) cucumbers, 1½–3 inches (3¾–7½ cm) long
½ cup (125 ml) pure, granulated salt
8 cups (2000 ml) sugar, divided
1½ quarts (1½ l) vinegar, divided
¾ teaspoon turmeric
2 teaspoons celery seed
2 teaspoons whole mixed pickling spices
8 cinnamon sticks, 1-inch (2½-cm) pieces
½ teaspoon fennel
2 teaspoons vanilla

First Day

1. Wash the cucumbers thoroughly. Scrub with a vegetable brush. Stem the ends that may be left on. Drain the cucumbers.
2. Place in a large container and cover with boiling water. After 6–8 hours, drain, and cover with fresh, boiling water.

Second Day

3. Drain the cucumbers, and cover with fresh, boiling water. After 6–8 hours, drain.
4. Add the salt and cover with fresh, boiling water.

Third Day

5. Drain the cucumbers. Prick the cucumbers in several places with a table fork.
6. Make a syrup of 3 cups (750 ml) sugar and 3 cups (750 ml) vinegar; add the turmeric and other spices. Heat to boiling and pour over the cucumbers. (Cucumbers will only be partially covered at this point.) After 6–8 hours, drain the syrup into a pan.
7. Add 2 cups (500 ml) sugar and 2 cups (500 ml) vinegar to the syrup and heat to boiling. Pour over the pickles.

Fourth Day

8. Drain the syrup into a pan. Add 2 cups (500 ml) sugar and 1 cup (250 ml) vinegar to the syrup and heat to boiling. Pour over the pickles. After 6–8 hours, drain the syrup into a pan.
9. Add the remaining cup of sugar and the vanilla to the syrup. Heat to boiling.
10. Pack the pickles into clean, hot pint jars and cover with boiling syrup to ½ inch from the top of the jar. Adjust the jar lids.
11. Process for 5 minutes (adjust for altitude according to the directions on page 216) in boiling water, starting to count as soon as the water returns to boiling.
12. Remove the jars and compete the seals, if necessary. Set the jars upright on a wire rack or folded towel to cool. Place them several inches apart.

Pickled Beets

3 quarts (2¾ l) beets, sliced
1 tablespoon whole allspice
2 cinnamon sticks
2 cups (500 ml) sugar
1½ teaspoons salt
3½ cups (875 ml) vinegar
1½ cups (375 ml) water

1. Wash the beets. Leave 2-inch (5-cm) stems and taproots. Cover with boiling water and cook whole until tender. Drain, peel, and slice.
2. Loosely tie the allspice and cinnamon sticks in a clean, thin, white cloth. Combine the sugar, salt, vinegar, and water in a kettle. Add the spice bag. Bring to a boil; cook slowly for 15 minutes.
3. Remove the spice bag. Pack the beets into hot, clean pint jars. Cover with the hot liquid, filling to ½ inch from the top. Adjust the jar lids.
4. Process in boiling water for 30 minutes (adjust for altitude according to the directions on page 216), starting to count as soon as the water returns to boiling. Remove the jars and compete the seals, if necessary. Set the jars upright on a wire rack or folded towel to cool. Place them several inches apart.

AMERICAN
KITCHEN KOOK
CLEANLINESS~SPEED~CONVENIENCE~ SAFETY

AMERICAN

Your Modern Kitchen Requires Kitchenkook

Easy-to-Make Relishes

Relishes for which ingredients are available throughout the year can be made in small quantities for use within 3 or 4 weeks. For such products, the boiling water bath process may be omitted, in which case the relish must be stored in the refrigerator. Two relishes that may be made in this way are horseradish relish and pepper-onion relish.

Horseradish Relish

2 cups (500 ml) grated horseradish
1 cup (250 ml) white vinegar
½ teaspoon salt

1. Wash the horseradish thoroughly and remove the brown outer skin. The roots may be grated or cut into small cubes and put through a food chopper.
2. Combine all the ingredients and pack into clean jars. Seal tightly and refrigerate.

Pepper-Onion Relish

1 quart (1 l) onion, finely chopped
2 cups (500 ml)sweet red pepper, finely chopped
2 cups (500 ml) green pepper, finely chopped
1 cup (250 ml) sugar
1 quart (1 l) vinegar
4 teaspoons salt

1. Combine all the ingredients in a kettle and bring to a boil. Boil gently for 45 minutes or until the mixture is thickened and reduced about one-half in volume, stirring occasionally.
2. Pack the boiling hot relish into clean, hot jars, filling to the top of jar. Seal tightly and refrigerate.

Note: If extended storage without refrigeration is desired, this product should be processed in a boiling water bath. Pack the boiling hot relish into clean, hot pint jars to ½ inch from the top of jar. Adjust the jar lids. Process in boiling water for 5 minutes (adjust for altitude according to the directions on page 216), starting to count as soon as the water returns to boiling. Remove the jars and compete the seals, if necessary. Set the jars upright on a wire rack or folded towel to cool. Place them several inches apart.

USDA Recommendations for Processing and Storing Pickles

Utensils

For heating pickling liquids, use utensils of unchipped enamelware, stainless steel, aluminum, or glass. Do not use copper, brass, galvanized, or iron utensils.

For fermenting or brining, use a leadfree crock or stone jar, unchipped enamel-lined pan, or large glass jar, bowl, or casserole. Use a heavy plate or large glass lid that fits inside the container to cover vegetables in brine. Use a weight to hold the cover down and keep vegetables below the surface of the brine. A glass jar filled with water makes a good weight.

A water-filled plastic bag is an effective cover for sealing the surface and keeping out air, thus preventing the growth of yeast or mold. The bag should be of heavyweight, watertight plastic and intended for use with food. Fill the bag with enough water to form a tight-fitting cover over the cabbage or cucumbers. Tie it tightly, and for added protection place the water-filled bag inside another heavyweight, watertight plastic bag intended for food use.

Small utensils that add ease and convenience to home pickling include: measuring spoons, large wood or stainless-steel spoons for stirring, measuring cups, sharp knives, large trays, tongs, vegetable peelers, ladle with a lip for pouring, slotted spoon, footed colander or wire basket, large-mouthed funnel, food chopper or grinder, and wood cutting board.

Water Bath Canner

Inexpensive enamelware canners may be purchased at most hardware or variety stores. However, any large metal container may be used, if it:

* Is deep enough to allow for 1–2 inches (2½–5 cm) of water above the tops of the jars, plus a little extra space for boiling (2–4 inches or 4–10 cm space above jars is ideal).
* Has a close fitting cover.
* Has a wire or wood rack with partitions to keep jars from touching each other or the bottom or sides of the container.

Glass Jars and Lids

Use jars specifically designed for home canning. Other jars may break more easily or not seal properly.

Select jars and lids that are free of cracks, chips, rust, dents, or any defect that may prevent airtight seals and cause needless spoilage. Select the size of lid, wide mouth or regular, that fits your jars.

Wash glass jars in hot, soapy water. Rinse thoroughly with hot water.

If two-piece lids are used, wash and rinse flat metal lids and metal screw bands. Always use new flat metal lids. These may have to be boiled or held in boiling water for a few minutes before they are used. Follow the manufacturer's directions.

For porcelain-lined zinc caps, use clean, new rubber rings of the right size for the jars. Do not test by stretching. Dip rubber rings in boiling water before putting them on the jars.

Filling Jars

Fill the jars firmly and uniformly with the product. Do not pack them so tightly that there is no room for the brine or syrup around and over the pickle. Be sure to leave headspace at the top of the jar.

Wipe the rim and threads of the jar with a clean, hot cloth to remove any particles of food, seeds, or spices. Even a small particle may prevent an airtight seal.

Closing Jars

The two-piece metal cap (flat metal lid and metal screw band) is the most commonly used closure. To use, place the lid on the jar with the sealing compound next to the glass. Screw the metal band down tight by hand to hold the sealing compound against the glass. When the band is closed tight, this lid has enough "give" to let air escape during processing. Do not tighten the screw band further after processing.

When using a porcelain-lined zinc cap with shoulder rubber ring, put the wet rubber ring on the jar shoulder before filling the jar. Do not stretch the rubber ring more than necessary. Screw the cap down firmly against the wet rubber ring, then turn it back one-fourth inch. Immediately after processing and removal of the jar from the canner, screw the cap down tight to complete the seal.

If liquid has boiled out of a jar during processing, do not open it to add more liquid, because spoilage organisms may enter. A loss of liquid does not cause food to spoil, if the lid is sealed properly.

Heat Treatment

Pickle products require heat treatment to destroy organisms that cause spoilage and to inactivate enzymes that may affect flavor, color, and texture. Adequate heating is best achieved by processing filled jars in a boiling water bath.

Pack pickle products into glass jars according to directions given in the recipe. Adjust lids. Immerse the jars in actively boiling water in canner or deep kettle. Be sure water comes an inch or two above the jar tops. Add boiling water, if necessary, but do not pour it directly on the jars.

Cover the container with a close-fitting lid and bring the water back to boiling as quickly as possible. Start to count processing time when the water returns to boiling, and continue to boil gently and steadily for the time recommended for the food being canned. Remove jars immediately and complete the seals if porcelain-lined zinc caps have been used. Set jars upright on a wire rack or folded towel to cool. Place them several inches apart. Keep out of draft. Do not cover jars.

Processing procedures for fermented cucumbers and fresh-pack dills are slightly different from the usual water bath process. For these products, start to count the processing time as soon as the filled jars are placed in the actively boiling water. This prevents development of a cooked flavor and loss of crispness.

Processing times vary by altitude. Increase processing time by 1 minute at 1,000 feet (300 m), and for each additional 1,000 feet or 300 m (i.e., 2,000 feet or 600 m, 2 additional minutes processing time; 3,000 feet or 900 m, 3 additional minutes, etc.).

Cooling Canned Pickles

Cool for 12–24 hours. Remove metal screw bands carefully, and check jars for an airtight seal. If the center of the lid has a slight dip or stays down when pressed, the jar is sealed. Another way to check for airtight seal is to turn the jar partly over. If there is no leakage, the jar may be stored.

If a porcelain-lined zinc cap with rubber ring has been used, check for airtight seal by turning the jar partly over. If there is no leakage, the seal is tight.

If a jar shows signs of leakage or poor seal, use the product right away or recan it by repacking in another clean jar and reprocessing as before.

Storing Canned Pickles

Wipe jars with a clean, damp cloth, and label with name of product and date. Store in a dark, dry, cool place where there is no danger of freezing.

Always be on the alert for signs of spoilage. A bulging lid; leakage; upon opening, spurting liquid; mold; odor; change in color; or an unusual softness, mushiness, or slipperiness. If there is any sign of spoilage, do not eat or even taste the contents. Dispose of contents so that they cannot be eaten by humans or animals.

Index

The FARMER'S WIFE
Magazine

JULY
1936